## Dear Student,

When you open *McDougal, Littell English,* you are beginning a journey. You will be traveling through the world of words. You will discover your own talent for shaping ideas into words.

*McDougal, Littell English* uses literature as your guide. Below is a list of some of the titles and authors of the literature you will read as models of good writing. Let those models lead you to the books themselves so that you can discover and enjoy the power of words in the world of literature.

The Editors

### Literary Selections in *McDougal, Littell English, Brown Level*

Aesop, "The Shepherd Boy and the Wolf." ▸*The Caldecott Aesop: Twenty Fables*
Aldis, Dorothy, "The Picnic," *Hop, Skip, and Jump!;* "Brooms," *Everything and Anything.* ▸*All Together*
Bacmeister, Rhoda, "Stars," "Galoshes," *Stories to Begin On.*
Chaikin, Miriam, "One-Upmanship." ▸*Aviva's Piano*
Chute, Marchette, "At the Library," *Rhymes About Us.* ▸*Around and About*
Cole, William, "Here Comes the Band." ▸*Oh, Such Foolishness!*
De Regniers, Beatrice Schenk, "Keep a Poem in Your Pocket," *Something Special.* ▸*May I Bring a Friend?*
Fallis, Edwina, "September," *Sung Under the Silver Umbrella.*
Farjeon, Eleanor, "There Isn't Time," "Verbs," "Down! Down!" *Eleanor Farjeon's Poems for Children.* ▸*The Children's Bells*
Fisher, Aileen, "My Cat," "How Big?" *Out in the Dark and Daylight;* "Spring," *Runny Days, Sunny Days.* ▸*Like Nothing at All*
Gardner, John, "The Lizard," *A Child's Bestiary.* ▸*Dragon, Dragon and Other Tales*
Gardner, Martin, "Magic Word," *Never Make Fun of a Turtle.* ▸*Mathematical Carnival*
Guiterman, Arthur, "Chums," *The Laughing Muse.*
Heide, Florence Parry, "Rocks." ▸*Banana Blitz*

(Continued on Page 356.)

# McDougal, Littell
# ENGLISH

Green Level
Red Level
Gold Level
Silver Level
Aqua Level
**BROWN LEVEL**
Plum Level
Pink Level
Cherry Level (K)

McDougal, Littell & Company

**Evanston, Illinois**

New York   Dallas   Sacramento   Raleigh

## Authors

**Frances Freeman Paden,** Ph.D., Lecturer, Department of English and Communicative Arts, Roosevelt University, Chicago, Illinois

**Susan Duffy Schaffrath,** Consultant in Educational Materials for the Elementary and Middle Grades, Chicago, Illinois

The Editorial Staff of McDougal, Littell & Company

## Consultants

Deborah Kay Bossmeyer, Middle School Team Leader and Language Arts Teacher, DuValle Middle School, Louisville, Kentucky

Patricia Brackenrich, Principal, White Sulphur Elementary School, White Sulphur Springs, West Virginia

Ann E. Davis, Assistant Superintendent, Washington County Education Service District, Portland, Oregon

Joy C. Fowles, Ph.D., Coordinator for Secondary Education, Clear Creek Independent School District, League City, Texas

Susan Vignes Hahn, Assistant Superintendent for Instruction, Archdiocese of San Francisco, San Francisco, California

Nana E. Hilsenbeck, Language Arts Supervisor, Volusia County School District, Daytona Beach, Florida

Edna W. Massingill, Assistant Principal, Clinton Park Elementary School, Clinton, Mississippi

James W. Reith, Program Coordinator for Language Arts, Foreign Languages, and Libraries, Scottsdale School District, Phoenix, Arizona

**Cover Art:** *A Bird Friend* by an elementary school student, courtesy of The International Collection of Children's Art, University Museums, Illinois State University.

WARNING: No part of this book may be reproduced or transmitted in any form or by any means, electronic or mechanical, including photocopying, recording, or by any information storage and retrieval system, without permission in writing from the Publisher.

**Acknowledgments:** See page 355

ISBN:0-8123-5054-3

Copyright © 1989, 1987 by McDougal, Littell & Company
Box 1667, Evanston, Illinois 60204
All rights reserved. Printed in the United States of America

# Contents

## Unit 1 The World of Words  2

**Speaking and Listening**

### Chapter 1  Becoming a Better Speaker and Listener  5

1. Making Introductions  6
2. Helping People Listen to You  8
3. Carrying on a Conversation  10
4. Talking on the Telephone  12
5. Taking a Message  14

   *Using English in Reading*  16

   CHAPTER REVIEW  17

**Vocabulary Skills**

### Chapter 2  Understanding How Language Grows  19

1. Words That Come from Sounds  20
2. Words from Other Languages  22
3. Short Words from Long Words  24
4. Building Compound Words  25
5. Using Prefixes  26
6. Using Suffixes  28

   *Using English in Art*  30

   CHAPTER REVIEW  31

**Research Skills**

### Chapter 3  Using the Dictionary  33

1. Finding a Word in the Dictionary  34
2. Using Guide Words  36
3. Finding the Meaning of a Word  38

| | | 4 | Synonyms | 40 |
| | | 5 | Antonyms | 42 |
| | | 6 | Finding Clues to Meanings | 44 |
| | | | *Using English in Spelling* | 46 |
| | | | **CHAPTER REVIEW** | **47** |

**Grammar**    Chapter 4    **Learning About Sentences**    **49**
With Applied Writing Activities

1. What Is a Sentence?    50
2. Kinds of Sentences    52
3. The Parts of the Sentence    54
4. Writing Better Sentences    56

*Exercises for Mastery*    58

*Using Grammar in Writing*    60

**CHAPTER REVIEW**    **61**

**Composition**    Chapter 5    **Writing Paragraphs**    **63**

1. Learning About Paragraphs    64
2. The Topic Sentence    66
3. Learning About Prewriting    68
4. Writing a Draft    70
5. Revising a Paragraph    72
6. Finishing and Sharing a Paragraph    74

*Speaking and Listening—Giving a Talk*    76

*Creative Writing*    77

*Using English in Science*    78

**CHAPTER REVIEW**    **79**

**CUMULATIVE REVIEW**    **80**

# Unit 2 Gathering Words into Ideas  82

**Grammar** — Chapter 6 — **Learning About Nouns**  85
**With Applied Writing Activities**

1. What Are Nouns?  86
2. Common Nouns and Proper Nouns  88
3. Singular Nouns and Plural Nouns  90
4. Making Nouns Show Possession  92

   *Exercises for Mastery*  94

   *Using Grammar in Writing*  96

   **CHAPTER REVIEW**  97

**Grammar** — Chapter 7 — **Learning About Pronouns**  99
**With Applied Writing Activities**

1. What Are Pronouns?  100
2. Using Pronouns as Subjects  102
3. Pronouns in Other Parts of the Sentence  104
4. Possessive Pronouns  106
5. Using *Its, It's, Their, There,* and *They're*  108

   *Exercises for Mastery*  110

   *Using Grammar in Writing*  112

   **CHAPTER REVIEW**  113

**Speaking and Listening** — Chapter 8 — **Telling a Story**  115

1. Discovering the Parts of a Story  116
2. Reading a Story Aloud  118
3. Telling a Story About Yourself  120
4. Telling a Class Story  122

   *Using English in Drama*  124

   **CHAPTER REVIEW**  125

**Grammar**

**Chapter 9  Learning About Verbs   127**
With Applied Writing Activities

    **1**  What Are Verbs?   128

    **2**  Two Kinds of Verbs   130

    **3**  Main Verbs and Helping Verbs   133

    **4**  Verbs That Tell About Present Time   136

    **5**  Verbs That Tell About Past Time   139

    **6**  More Verbs That Change Their Form   142

    **7**  Using Contractions   144

    **8**  Using Negatives Correctly   147

       *Exercises for Mastery*   148

       *Using Grammar in Writing*   152

       **CHAPTER REVIEW**   153

**Composition**

**Chapter 10  Writing A Story   155**

    **1**  Thinking About Stories   156

    **2**  Parts of a Story   158

    **3**  Planning and Writing a Story   160

    **4**  Revising and Sharing a Story   162

       *Speaking and Listening—Giving a Puppet Show*   164

       *Creative Writing*   165

       *Using English in Social Studies*   166

       **CHAPTER REVIEW**   167

**CUMULATIVE REVIEW**   168

# Unit 3 Sharing Secrets 170

**Grammar**    Chapter 11    **Learning About Adjectives and Adverbs**    173
With Applied Writing Activities

1. What Are Adjectives?    174
2. Kinds of Adjectives    176
3. Using *A*, *An*, and *The*    179
4. Using Adjectives to Compare    180
5. What Are Adverbs?    183

*Exercises for Mastery*    186

*Using Grammar in Writing*    188

**CHAPTER REVIEW**    189

**Composition**    Chapter 12    **Writing a Description**    191

1. Thinking About Describing    192
2. Planning and Writing a Description    194
3. Revising and Sharing a Description    196

*Speaking and Listening—Listening for Sounds*    198

*Creative Writing*    199

*Using English in Science*    200

**CHAPTER REVIEW**    201

**Literature Skills**    Chapter 13    **Discovering Poetry**    203

1. What Is a Poem?    204
2. Seeing Pictures in a Poem    206
3. Hearing the Sounds in a Poem    208
4. Feeling the Rhythm of a Poem    210

*Using English in Art*    212

**CHAPTER REVIEW**    213

**Speaking and Listening** — **Chapter 14** **Giving and Following Directions**    **215**

    **1** Giving Directions to Others    216

    **2** Following Written Directions    218

    **3** Listening to Oral Directions    220

    **4** Following Test Directions    222

    *Using English in Health and Safety*    224

    CHAPTER REVIEW    225

**Composition** — **Chapter 15** **Writing To Explain How**    **227**

    **1** Thinking About Explaining How    228

    **2** Planning and Writing a *How* Paragraph    230

    **3** Revising and Sharing a *How* Paragraph    232

    *Speaking and Listening—Giving a Talk To Tell How*    234

    *Creative Writing*    235

    *Using English in Health*    236

    CHAPTER REVIEW    237

**CUMULATIVE REVIEW**    238

## Unit 4 Searching    240

**Composition** — **Chapter 16** **Writing Friendly Letters**    **243**

    **1** Writing a Friendly Letter    244

    **2** Addressing an Envelope    248

    **3** Writing an Invitation    250

    **4** Writing a Thank-You Note    252

    *Using English in Cursive Writing*    254

    CHAPTER REVIEW    255

## Thinking Skills

### Chapter 17  Thinking Clearly   257

1. Facts and Opinions   258
2. Forming an Opinion   260
3. Generalizations   263
   *Using English in Math*   266
   CHAPTER REVIEW   267

## Research Skills

### Chapter 18  Getting To Know the Library   269

1. Kinds of Books   270
2. Using the Card Catalog   272
3. The Parts of a Book   274
4. Using an Encyclopedia   276
   *Using English in Social Studies*   278
   CHAPTER REVIEW   279

## Composition

### Chapter 19  Writing a Report   281

1. Thinking About Reports   282
2. Prewriting: Choosing a Subject and Taking Notes   284
3. Making a Plan and Writing a Draft   286
4. Revising and Sharing a Report   288
   *Speaking and Listening—An Interview*   290
   *Creative Writing*   291
   *Using English in Reading*   292
   CHAPTER REVIEW   293

## Grammar

### Chapter 20  Using Capital Letters   295

1. Names of People and Pets   296
2. Particular Places and Things   298
3. First Words   300

    **4**  Titles    302

        *Exercises for Mastery*    304

        *Using Grammar in Writing*    306

        CHAPTER REVIEW    307

**Grammar**      Chapter 21    **Using Punctuation Marks**    309

    **1**  The Period    310

    **2**  The Question Mark    312

    **3**  The Exclamation Point    313

    **4**  The Comma    314

    **5**  More About the Comma    316

    **6**  The Apostrophe    318

    **7**  Quotation Marks    320

    **8**  Writing Book Titles    321

        *Exercises for Mastery*    322

        *Using Grammar in Writing*    324

        CHAPTER REVIEW    325

**CUMULATIVE REVIEW**    326

## *Power Handbook*    329

**Composition**    Guides for the Process of Writing    330

**Composition**    Topics for Writing    333

**Grammar**    Guide to Spelling    336

**Vocabulary Research**    Word Bank for Writers    341

# UNIT 1

Chapter 1    **Becoming a Better Speaker and Listener**
Chapter 2    **Understanding How Language Grows**
Chapter 3    **Using the Dictionary**
Chapter 4    **Learning About Sentences**
Chapter 5    **Writing Paragraphs**

## *The World of Words*

In Unit 1, you will begin to discover more about your language. You will learn skills you need to speak and write better than you ever have before.

First, you will study ways to be a good speaker and listener. You will learn about words that make up our language. You will use words to write sentences. You will use the sentences to build a paragraph.

Your new skills will be helpful in all of your school subjects. They will help you find the meaning of a new word when you are reading. You will be able to write better paragraphs in science and social studies. You will know how to express your ideas clearly.

This is just the beginning of your journey through the world of words. There are always new words to learn. There are always new ideas to share. It is a journey that never ends.

## THERE ISN'T TIME

There isn't time, there isn't time
To do the things I want to do,
With all the mountain-tops to climb,
And all the woods to wander through,
And all the seas to sail upon,
And everywhere there is to go,
And all the people, every one
Who lives upon the earth, to know.
There's only time, there's only time
To know a few, and do a few,
And then sit down and make a rhyme
About the rest I want to do.

—ELEANOR FARJEON

# Chapter 1

# Becoming a Better Speaker and Listener

Have you ever tried not to talk for an hour or even ten minutes? You can hardly keep quiet. You feel like you are going to burst.

When you try not to talk, you find out how important talking is. It is the most important way we have to share our ideas. Listening is important, too. It is the main way we receive ideas from others.

In this chapter, you will learn some things that will help you become a better speaker. You will learn some ways to be a better listener, too.

# 1 Making Introductions

> When you introduce people, remember these things.
> 1. Look at the people you are introducing.
> 2. Say the names of each person.
> 3. Tell something about each person.

You often speak to two or more people at the same time. Sometimes they may not know each other. You may need to introduce them.

José's mother has come to Parent's Day at school. She has never met his teacher. Let's see how José introduces his mother to his teacher.

> "Mrs. Davis, I'd like you to meet my mother, Mrs. Fernández."
>
> Then José turns to his mother. He says, "Mom, this is my teacher, Mrs. Davis. She has been helping me learn to write better."

First, José presented his mother to his teacher. He introduced his mother by saying her name. Next, José introduced his teacher, Mrs. Davis. He also told his mother something about his teacher.

You should always say more than names when you introduce people. Try to think of something interesting to say about each person. This will make it easier for people to start talking.

# Exercises  Making Introductions

**A.** Carol wants her friend Laura to meet her other friends. Read Carol's introduction. Then answer the questions below the box.

> "Amy! Benjamin! I want you to meet my new neighbor, Laura. She just moved here from Florida."
>
> (Then Carol turns to Laura and speaks.)
>
> "Laura, these are my friends. Benjamin lives on our street. Amy and I are in the same class at school."

1. Whom did Carol want Laura to meet?
2. What did Carol say about Laura?
3. What did Carol tell Laura about her friends?

**B.** Work in groups of four. Act out one of the following introductions.

1. Wanda's cousin Brian is visiting her. Wanda's friend Theo Pappas invites them to play at his house. Wanda introduces Brian to Theo and his father, Mr. Pappas.

2. This is Angelo's first day of school. The only person he knows is Diana. Diana greets Angelo. Then she introduces him to her friends, Ed and Tina.

## 2 Helping People Listen to You

> The way you speak can help people listen to you.

Sometimes people don't listen because of the way a speaker is talking. You can help your listeners by being a thoughtful speaker. Here are some ways to help people listen to you.

**Guides for Helping People Listen to You**

1. Keep your mind on what you are saying.
2. Speak clearly.
3. Let your actions follow your thoughts.
4. Look into your listener's eyes.
5. Make your voice pleasant.

This picture shows Peggy talking about her new kitten. She is using her hands to show the kitten's size and actions. Her face shows that she is happy to have the kitten.

Peggy is thinking hard about what she is saying. She is looking at her audience. She is speaking clearly in a pleasant voice.

## Exercises — Helping People Listen to You

**A.** Read these sentences. First, read them in a complaining or shouting voice. Then read the sentences in a pleasant voice. Let others tell if they can hear the difference.

1. Mom, Peter took my ball and glove. He won't give them back.
2. I dusted the erasers yesterday. Sandra should do it today.
3. Leroy already had five turns. He should let each of us have a turn.

**B.** Form groups to act out the following scenes. Have listeners tell what is wrong in each scene.

1. Mrs. Wall says hello to Kevin. He is shy. He looks at his feet and says hello.
2. Carmen is giving a talk about the circus. She doesn't look at her listeners. Instead, she stares at the floor.

**C.** Take turns acting out the scenes in Exercise B one more time. This time speak clearly and look at your listeners. Practice helping people listen to you.

# 3 Carrying on a Conversation

> When you are having a conversation, listen carefully, answer politely, and ask questions.

Once people know something about each other, they usually begin to talk. However, carrying on a conversation is not always easy. You must keep your mind on what people are saying. It is important to listen and ask questions.

Read this conversation among three friends.

SONYA: I have some new roller skates. I can't wait to try them.
TODD: Do you know how to skate?
SONYA: I learned last summer. Ever since then, I've wanted skates.
VAL: Could we go skating on Saturday afternoon?
SONYA: That would be fun. I'll ask my dad.
TODD: I will, too. I don't have skates, but I think I can borrow my brother's.
VAL: I'll ask my parents. I'm sure it will be okay. Let's meet again tomorrow. We can make plans then.

In this conversation, everyone took turns. Two questions helped to keep the conversation going.

The following guides will help you have good conversations.

**Guides for Carrying on a Conversation**

1. Let each person talk.
2. Ask questions.
3. Add new ideas.
4. Listen to others.
5. Be friendly.

## Exercise  Carrying on a Conversation

Read this conversation. Then answer the questions below.

NINA: My goldfish aren't doing very well.
YOSHI: Maybe you need to clean their bowl.
JERRY: You never take care of your animals, Nina.
NINA: Yes, I do. Does anyone know if fish need vitamins?
YOSHI: Sometimes they need a special food. Mr. Lerman can tell you about that.
NINA: I'll go to see him after school.
JERRY: I'm tired of hearing about your fish.

1. Which person is not being friendly?
2. Who listens and then asks a question?
3. If you joined the group, what new idea would you talk about?

## 4 Talking on the Telephone

> When you use the telephone, be sure to speak clearly. Listen carefully to what the caller is saying.

Sometimes your conversations take place on the telephone. Of course, on the phone you and your friends can't see each other. You must speak and listen very carefully to keep the message clear.

Here's what happens when the phone rings in Tony's house.

TONY: Hello.

VOICE: Hello. This is Jeff. May I speak with Tony, please?

TONY: Hi, Jeff. This is Tony.

JEFF: Hi, Tony. Can you go to the park with me?

TONY: Just a minute, please. I'll ask Mom.

(Tony puts the receiver down gently. He asks his mother for permission to go to the park. Then he returns to the phone.)

Jeff? Mom says okay. I'll meet you there in ten minutes.

JEFF: Great! See you then, Tony.

TONY: Goodbye, Jeff.

JEFF: Goodbye.

Tony and Jeff were polite to each other. What did Tony say when he had to leave the phone? How did he set the phone down? Remember to use your best manners on the telephone.

These guides will help you talk with others on the telephone.

**Guides for Talking on the Telephone**

1. When you pick up the phone, say "Hello."
2. If you are the caller, give your name. Tell why you are calling.
3. Listen carefully.
4. Speak clearly.
5. Say "Goodbye" before you hang up.

## Exercise   Talking on the Telephone

Work in groups of four. Take turns acting out one of these phone calls. Be sure to follow the guides above. When it is not your turn to act, listen to the others.

1. Emily calls Ira. She wants to go to Ira's house. She wants to return a record she borrowed from him.
2. Maria calls Sarah. She wants to invite Sarah to stay overnight. Sarah must get her mother's permission.
3. Carlos calls Greg. Carlos wants to play ball. He asks Greg to meet him at school.

After you have acted out your phone call, ask your group to tell you how you did.

# 5 Taking a Message

> When you take a message, listen carefully.
> Repeat the message to be sure it is right.

Sometimes you need to take a telephone message. Listen carefully. Write the name of the person who should get the message. Write the message. Repeat the message to make sure it is right. Sign your name.

Here is a telephone conversation. Tanya is home alone when the phone rings.

TANYA: Hello.
VOICE: Hello. This is Mr. Steel at the service station. May I speak to Mr. Gibson?
TANYA: He can't come to the phone now. May I take a message?
MR. STEEL: Yes, thank you. Mr. Gibson's car is ready to be picked up.
TANYA: All right, Mr. Steel. I'll tell my father that his car is ready.
MR. STEEL: Thank you. Goodbye.
TANYA: Goodbye.

When the caller asked to speak to Tanya's father, Tanya said, "He can't come to the phone now." For safety reasons, never tell strangers that your parents are not at home. Just take the message politely.

Look at the message that Tanya wrote. She told whom the message is for. She signed her name.

> Dear Dad,
>  Mr. Steel from the service station called. He said your car is ready.
>  Tanya

## Exercises  Taking a Telephone Message

**A.** Write telephone messages for the following calls. Tell who gets the message and who called. Sign your name.

1. Your mother calls you from work. She wants you to remind your sister Sally to go to the dentist. Her appointment is at 4:00 p.m.

2. Your older brother Dan calls. He asks you to tell your mother he won't be home for dinner. He is eating at his friend's house. His friend is Marco Báez.

3. Mr. Tillman calls from the hardware store. Your father ordered a new screen. It can be delivered tomorrow. Mr. Tillman would like your father to call him at the store.

**B.** Practice taking telephone messages with a partner. Take turns being a caller and a message-taker. One person should call and leave a message. The other person should answer and write the message.

# Using English in Reading

You can share a good book with your friends. One way is to talk about it. When you talk about a book, tell these four important things: the title, the author, what the book is about, and why you liked it. Study this picture of two people talking about a book.

**Exercises**  **Talking About a Book**

**A.** In the conversation above, you learned four things about a book. Answer these questions to show what you learned.

1. What is the title of the book?
2. Who is the author?
3. What is the book about?
4. Why did the person like the book?

**B.** Choose a book to share with a classmate. Tell the four important things about the book.

# Chapter 1 Review

**A. Rules for Speaking and Listening** There is a word missing in each of these rules. Use a word from the list to complete each rule. Write the sentences.

message   ideas   introduce   eyes   clearly
person    voice   questions   mind   interrupt

1. Keep your _____ on what you are saying.
2. When you take a _____, listen carefully.
3. Talk in a pleasant _____.
4. Do not _____ when someone else is talking.
5. Ask _____ to keep a conversation going.
6. Tell your name to the _____ you call.
7. Look into your listeners' _____.
8. When two people do not know each other, it is good to _____ them.
9. Speak _____ on the phone or in person.
10. Add new _____ to the conversation.

**B. Taking a Telephone Message** Read about two telephone calls. Write a message for each call.

1. Mr. Novak calls your father. Your father is at work. Mr. Novak wants to borrow your ladder on Saturday. Write the message to your father.

2. Your neighbor Mrs. Keeler calls. She has to take her dog to the doctor. Your brother Bill walks her dog after school. She asks you to tell Bill that he doesn't have to walk the dog. Write the message to Bill.

# Chapter 2

# Understanding How Language Grows

We see growing things all around us. New flowers bloom. Branches grow on trees. Babies grow taller and learn to speak. All living things grow and change.

Just as people and plants grow, so does language. New words come into the English language every day. Here are some ways we add and change words.

> We borrow words from other languages.
> We make words out of sounds.
> We put two words together to make one word.
> We cut or "clip" a word to make it shorter.
> We add parts to the beginning or end of words.

In this chapter, you will look at words that have come into our language. You will see that a growing language is an exciting language.

# 1 Words That Come from Sounds

> Many words in our language come from sounds. These words are called **echoic words**.

Say the word *pop* out loud. It echoes a real sound. When you make popcorn, you hear the *pop* sound. When you break a balloon, you hear a *pop*.

The word *growl* also echoes a real sound. A lion may growl. An angry dog often growls. Words like *pop* and *growl* are called **echoic words**.

Now say the following echoic words aloud. Listen to the sound of each word. Think of something that makes each sound.

| | | |
|---|---|---|
| hum | thump | crunch |
| swish | buzz | gurgle |

🗝 **Key to Writing and Speaking** Echoic words are fun to use. The reader or listener "hears" what the words mean.

## Exercises  Using Echoic Words

**A.** Match each sound in the first list to an echoic word in the second list. Write the sounds and the echoic words.

1. the sound of a duck
2. the sound of thunder
3. the sound of a blazing fire
4. the sound of a loud bell
5. the sound of cloth tearing
6. the sound of a happy cat
7. the sound of a car horn
8. the sound of a bubbly soda
9. the sound of a bee
10. the sound of an angry cat

a. boom
b. crackle
c. rip
d. quack
e. fizz
f. purr
g. clang
h. honk
i. hiss
j. buzz

**B.** Read these sentences aloud. Listen for one echoic word in each sentence. Write the echoic words.

1. The horses went clip-clop as they marched by.
2. Bob's parrot squawks at visitors.
3. The water went ping every time it dripped.
4. The city bus whizzed by.
5. Our floor creaks when we walk on it.
6. The rock splashed as it fell in the water.
7. Mom's sewing machine hummed as she sewed.
8. The jet whistled above.
9. My shoes made a thud as they hit the floor.
10. Do you like to hear the strum of a guitar?

**C. Speaking and Listening** Take turns saying echoic words. The listeners can guess what the sounds stand for. Here are some echoic words you can use: *bong, squeal, squish.*

# 2 Words from Other Languages

> Many of our words come from other languages. These words are called **borrowed words**.

The English language borrows words from other languages. Some of these languages are Spanish, French, Italian, Dutch, German, American Indian, and African.

When the first settlers came to America, they learned many words from the Native Americans. The settlers learned the Indian names for trees, fruits, and vegetables.

Since that time, people from all over the world have come to our country. Each group of people brought a whole new set of words. Many of those words became part of the English language.

These nine food words came from other countries. Can you guess where each word came from?

| | | |
|---|---|---|
| won ton | spaghetti | frankfurter |
| taco | chili | crepe |
| strudel | pizza | gumbo |

  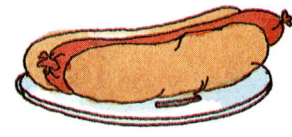

Look at the chart on the next page. It gives some examples of words borrowed from other languages.

| American Indian | Spanish/ Mexican | French |
|---|---|---|
| canoe | ranch | pumpkin |
| skunk | rodeo | magic |
| moose | patio | ballet |
| coyote | armadillo | button |
| **Dutch** | **German** | **African** |
| freight | dachshund | banjo |
| easel | pretzel | okra |
| landscape | delicatessen | gnu |
| stoop | kindergarten | marimba |

## Exercises  Using Borrowed Words

**A.** Here are the names of five animals. The names are all borrowed words. Look at the chart. Decide which language each word came from.

1. coyote
2. dachshund
3. armadillo
4. gnu
5. moose

**B.** Find a borrowed word to fit each sentence. Use the chart at the top of the page. Write the sentences.

1. Jan lost the paddle for her _____.
2. My aunt raises horses on her _____.
3. Gary went to _____ when he was five.
4. A _____ train takes coal to the city.
5. Dad carved our _____ for Halloween.

# 3 Short Words from Long Words

> Some new words are made by shortening longer words. The new short word is called a **clipped word**.

New words do not always come from other languages. Sometimes our own language gives us new words. Did you know that the word *zoo* comes from the phrase *zoological garden*? We cut off, or clipped, part of a longer word. *Zoo* is a **clipped word**. Look at these other examples of clipped words.

    hamburger—burger
    submarine—sub

### Exercise  Making Clipped Words from Longer Words

Here are the long forms of ten words. Write the clipped form of each word.

1. photograph
2. telephone
3. frankfurter
4. mathematics
5. gymnasium
6. taxicab
7. milkshake
8. automobile
9. airplane
10. chimpanzee

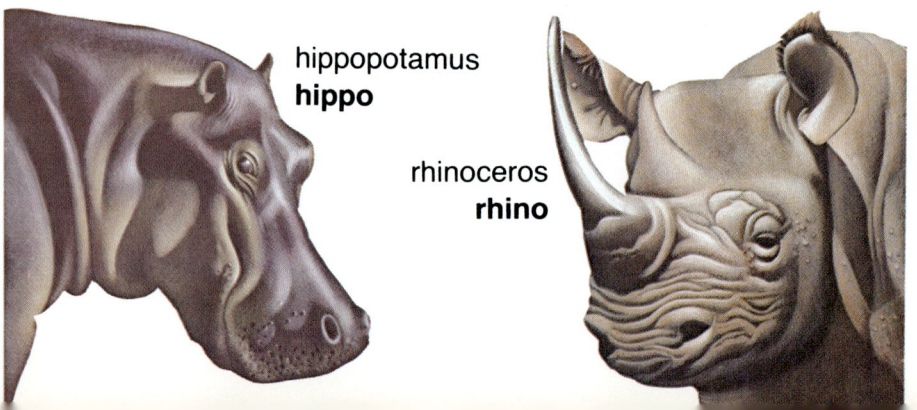

hippopotamus
**hippo**

rhinoceros
**rhino**

# 4 Building Compound Words

> Two words can be put together to make a new word. The new word is called a **compound word**.

Some words in our language are "built" from other words. Two words can be put together to become one word. The new word is called a **compound word.** *Football* came from *foot* and *ball*. Here is another example of a compound word.

flower     pot                    flowerpot

Compound words are added to the English language all the time. When a machine that washes dishes was invented, it was called a *dishwasher*.

## Exercises   Making Compound Words

**A.** Here are two sets of words. Match the words in each set to make compound words. Write the compound words.

| | | | | | |
|---|---|---|---|---|---|
| 1. | tree | ball | 1. | tooth | box |
| 2. | base | top | 2. | play | brush |
| 3. | sail | corn | 3. | toe | ground |
| 4. | door | boat | 4. | bed | nail |
| 5. | pop | knob | 5. | sand | room |

**B. Writing** You have invented a new machine. Tell what it does. Use a compound word to name your invention.

# 5 Using Prefixes

> A **prefix** is a word part added to the beginning of a word.

Another way to build a new word is to add a word part to the beginning of a word. The part that is added is called a **prefix**. A prefix changes the meaning of a word. Look at this example.

| Prefix | + | Word | = | New Word |
|--------|---|------|---|----------|
| re     |   | do   |   | redo     |

Adding the part *re-* to *do* makes a new word, *redo*. The prefix *re-* means "again." What does *redo* mean?

Here is another example of how *re-* builds a new word. What does *retie* mean?

Maria must *tie* the package.
Maria must *retie* the package.

The prefix *un-* means "not." Read this example of how the prefix *un-* builds a new word.

Jim is *happy*.
Jim is *unhappy*.

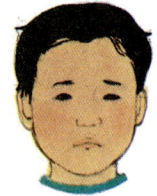

In the second sentence, Jim is "not happy." The prefix *un-* changed the meaning of the word *happy*. It also changed the meaning of the sentence.

# Exercises   Using Prefixes To Build Words

**A.** Write a new word that means the same as each pair of words. Use the prefix **re-** or **un-** in each new word.

1. not tied
2. wrap again
3. not planned
4. write again
5. run again
6. not finished
7. not clear
8. built again
9. not opened
10. fill again

unpack                    repack

**B.** Here are five sets of sentences. Write the second one of each set. Fill in the blanks. Use a prefix in each new word.

1. Dan's bike is not locked.
   Dan's bike is _____.

2. I will build the model again.
   I will _____ the model.

3. The frozen pizza is not cooked.
   The frozen pizza is _____.

4. My new desk is not painted.
   My new desk is _____.

5. Rosa wants to use the ribbon again.
   Rosa wants to _____ the ribbon.

# 6 Using Suffixes

> A **suffix** is a word part added to the end of a word.

Another way to build a new word is to add a word part at the end of a word. The part that is added is called a **suffix**. A suffix changes the meaning of a word. Look at this example.

| Word | + | Suffix | = | New Word |
|------|---|--------|---|----------|
| paint |  | er |  | painter |

The suffix -er means "a person who does something." What does *painter* mean?

Here is another example of how -er builds a new word. What does *trainer* mean?

My grandfather *trains* dogs.
My grandfather is a *trainer*.

The suffix -less means "without." Read this example of how it is used.

The old dog lost its last tooth.
The old dog was toothless.

The first sentence used *tooth* in a way you know. The second sentence says the dog was "without" a tooth. The suffix -less changed the meaning of *tooth*.

# Exercises  Using Suffixes To Build Words

**A.** Write a new word that means the same as each group of words below. Use the suffix **-er** or **-less** in your new word.

1. someone who climbs
2. without a home
3. without fear
4. someone who listens
5. without end
6. without use
7. someone who works
8. someone who reads
9. without hope
10. someone who farms

**B.** Here are five sets of sentences. Write the second sentence in each set. Fill in the blanks. Use a suffix for each new word.

1. Mrs. Ray is someone who teaches.
   Mrs. Ray is a _____.
2. Ben came without his cap.
   Ben was _____.
3. Someone who speaks is coming to our health class.
   A _____ is coming to our health class.
4. We ate chicken that had no bones.
   We ate _____ chicken.
5. Someone who prints needs a pencil.
   A _____ needs a pencil.

# Using English in Art

It is interesting to look at words we use in art. Some have been borrowed from other languages. Others are compound words or echoic words. We also add prefixes and suffixes to build new words.

**Exercise** **Using Words in Art**

Here are ten art words. Each word is either borrowed, echoic, compound, or built from a prefix or a suffix. Find a word to complete each sentence. Write the sentences.

marker swishing collage
repaste paintbrush orange
woodcuts watercolors easel
blue

1. If a thing needs to be pasted again, we _____ it.
2. We borrowed the Dutch word *ezel* for _____. It is a frame or stand to hold our pictures.
3. When you stir paints, you hear a _____ sound.
4. Something used to make marks is a _____.
5. _____ are paints made from water and colors.
6. The brush we paint pictures with is a _____.
7. *Naranja* is the Spanish word for the color _____.
8. Our word _____ comes from the French *bleu*.
9. The class gathered things to make a _____. It comes from the Greek word *kalla*.
10. At the museum, we saw pictures cut or carved from wood. They are called _____.

# Chapter 2 Review

**A. Echoic Words and Borrowed Words** Each sentence has an underlined word. Tell if the word is **echoic** or **borrowed.**

1. The French word for ax is *hache*.
2. Our puppy slurped its water.
3. The baby bird peeped as it waited for food.
4. The name for potato in Spain is *patata*.
5. A railroad engine chugs along the tracks.

**B. Words from Other Words** Each sentence has an underlined word. Tell if the word is **compound** or **clipped.**

1. Dad built a treehouse in the yard.
2. A submarine is often called a sub.
3. I saw a beautiful bluebird at the park.
4. Pam spent a day on her cousin's sailboat.
5. Mom buys gas at a gasoline station.

**C. Using Prefixes and Suffixes** Write the ten words listed below. Underline the prefix or suffix in each word. Then write what each word means.

Example: read<u>er</u>    someone who reads

1. unhurt
2. rewrite
3. unable
4. painless
5. farmer
6. remake
7. leader
8. unkind
9. singer
10. hairless

# Chapter 3

# Using the Dictionary

Where might you find a *dulcimer?* Would you look in a zoo or in a music store? When you are not sure what a word means, you can find the meaning in the dictionary.

A dictionary lists words in a language. You can learn about a new word by looking in a dictionary. You can learn how to spell the word and how to say it. You can learn what it means. Some words have several different meanings.

In this chapter, you will learn how to use the dictionary. It will help you discover the meanings of many new words.

# 1 Finding a Word in the Dictionary

> A dictionary lists words in **alphabetical order.**

A dictionary lists the words in a language. The words are listed in **alphabetical order.** Words beginning with *A* are first. *B* words come next. Then come *C* words, and so on.

When the first letters are the same, the order depends on the next letter. Look at these groups of words. They are in alphabetical order.

| 1 apple | 2 airplane | 3 crab |
|---|---|---|
| banana | apple | crib |
| cherry | ax | crutch |

Words beginning with the letters *A* through *M* are in the front half of the dictionary. *N* through *Z* words are in the back half of the dictionary.

Where would you look for a word that starts with *T*? Where would you look for these words?

    forest    spoon    derby    pantry

**Exercises**  **Finding a Word in the Dictionary**

**A.** Here are three lists of words. Write each list in alphabetical order. Remember, when the first letter is the same, look at the next letter to put the words in order.

1. animal
   fish
   bird
   person
   insect

2. desk
   day
   drill
   do
   dial

3. shine
   sun
   snow
   Saturday
   ski

**B.** Look at the words below. Where would you find these words in the dictionary? Write **Front** or **Back.**

1. port
2. beak
3. energy
4. tractor
5. harness
6. craft
7. argue
8. zest
9. weasel
10. draft
11. glare
12. vessel
13. knot
14. otter
15. stem

**C.** The dictionary is not the only book that uses alphabetical order. Telephone books also use it. The names of people are listed in alphabetical order, *last names first*.

Here is a list of five names. Write them in the order you would find them in a telephone book.

Arnold Long
Mary Santini
Daniel Brooks
Stella Cook
Thomas Morgan

# 2 Using Guide Words

> **Guide words** can help you find words in the dictionary.

Look at these two sample dictionary pages. The words in heavy type at the top of each page are called **guide words**. The guide word on the left of the page tells you the first word on that page. The guide word on the right tells you the last word on that page. On which page would you find the word *best*?

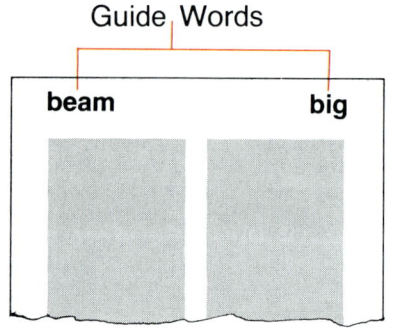
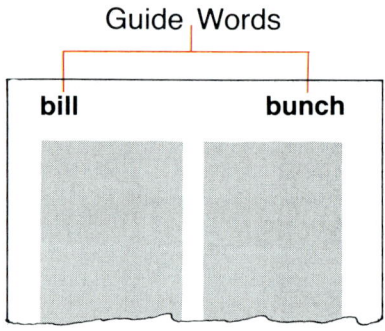

*Best* would be on the page with the guide words *beam* and *big*. *Best* comes between *beam* and *big* in alphabetical order.

On which page would you find these words?

    bend    bird    bump    break    bib

When you look for a word in the dictionary, the guide words can help you. Find the page with guide words closest in alphabetical order to your word. You will find the word you need on that page.

## Exercises  Using Guide Words

**A.** Look at the guide words on this page of a dictionary. Find six words in the list below that belong on this page. Write those words.

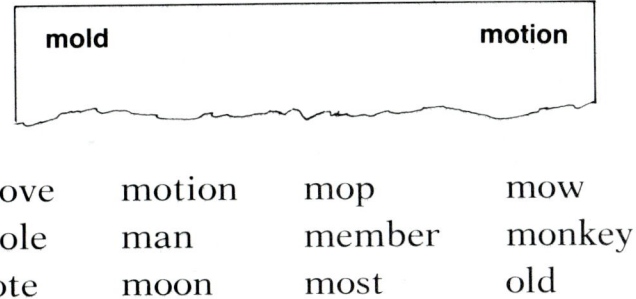

| | | | |
|---|---|---|---|
| move | motion | mop | mow |
| mole | man | member | monkey |
| note | moon | most | old |

**B.** After each of the following words, there are two pairs of guide words. Read each word. Choose the pair of guide words that will be on the page with that word. Write the guide words you have chosen.

1. beetle    beckon—before    bass—batter
2. circle    chubby—circle    civil—clap
3. grace    greeting—grind    grab—graft
4. football    fond—for    forge—form
5. tent    temple—tender    tendon—term

**C.** Use your class dictionary or one in the school library. Find the words listed below. Write the guide words from the top of each page.

1. piano
2. debate
3. market
4. extra
5. highway
6. shuttle

# 3 Finding the Meaning of a Word

> The dictionary tells the **meanings** of words.
> The **entry words** are printed in heavy black letters.
> The meanings are in lighter letters after the word.

Here is part of a dictionary page. The words in heavy type are called **entry words**. The dictionary uses more than one way to explain their meanings.

**has·sock** a firm cushion used as a footstool or low seat.
**haste 1.** the act of hurrying; quick movement or action [She left in *haste*.] **2.** a hurrying in a careless way [*Haste* makes waste.]
**hast·y** done or made with haste; hurried.
**hat** a head covering, usually with a brim and a crown.
**hatch 1.** to bring forth young birds, fish, turtles, from eggs **2.** to come forth from the egg **3.** to think up or plan, often in a secret or bad way.
**hatch·er·y** a place for hatching eggs, as of fish or hens.
**hatch·et** a small ax with a short handle.

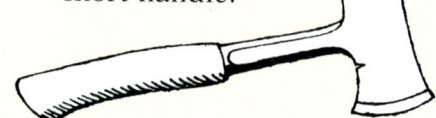

1. The dictionary simply tells the meaning of the word **hassock**.

2. Sample sentences help to make the meaning of **haste** clearer.

3. The dictionary has three meanings for **hatch**. Each meaning has a number. Choose the meaning that fits your sentence best.

4. The picture helps explain the meaning of **hatchet**.

**Exercises**  **Finding the Meaning of a Word**

**A.** A word is missing in each sentence below. Choose a word from the sample dictionary page on page 38. Make sure the word meaning fits each sentence. Write the sentence.

1. Grandmother rested her feet on a _____.
2. Peter chopped wood with a _____.
3. Robins _____ their eggs in the spring.
4. I painted carelessly because of my _____.
5. Fish are raised for food at the _____.
6. Don't do a _____ job if you want clean dishes.

**B.** Each of the following sentences uses a different meaning of *hatch*. For each sentence, choose the best meaning of *hatch* from the sample dictionary page. Write the number of the best meaning after the number of the sentence.

1. The pirates met to <u>hatch</u> a plan of action.

2. Turtles <u>hatch</u> their eggs by burying them in warm sand.

3. The father penguin holds the egg on his feet until it <u>hatches</u>.

# 4 Synonyms

> **Synonyms** are words that have the same or almost the same meaning.

Different words can have almost the same meaning. We call these words **synonyms**. Look at these word pairs. For each pair, the word on the left means almost the same as the word on the right.

call—shout          cold—chilly
little—tiny         take—grab
happy—cheerful      cry—weep

Often there is more than one word that says what you mean. Choose the word that says exactly what you want to say. Here are some synonyms for *large*.

vast    huge    mighty

Now look at the following sentences. Which synonym for *large* fits each sentence best?

We made a _____ snowman.
The wind blew across the _____ desert.

The dictionary sometimes gives synonyms for words. The synonyms are usually given after the meanings.

Another place to find synonyms is a **thesaurus**. Look at the **Word Bank for Writers** beginning on page 341. It is a kind of thesaurus. You will find synonyms for words you use often for your writing.

**Exercises   Finding and Using Synonyms**

**A.** Write the words in List 1. Next to each word, write its synonym from List 2.

| List 1 | List 2 |
|---|---|
| 1. throw | tardy |
| 2. giggle | pull |
| 3. late | skinny |
| 4. dark | leap |
| 5. tug | toss |
| 6. scream | burst |
| 7. thin | gloomy |
| 8. break | laugh |
| 9. jump | neat |
| 10. tidy | yell |

**B.** Choose the best word to complete each sentence. Use your dictionary if you need help. Write the sentences.

1. Lavon couldn't _____ the key in the lock.
    (spin, turn, whirl)

2. Edith heard a _____ on the door.
    (knock, swat, hit)

3. Which is the _____ to the balcony?
    (path, way, route)

4. The mail carrier had to _____ the package.
    (supply, give, deliver)

5. César wanted to _____ the band.
    (lead, steer, guide)

# 5 Antonyms

> **Antonyms** are words that have opposite meanings.

Look at these pairs of words.

    hot—cold        tall—short
    big—small      up—down

Each word on the left means the opposite of the word on the right. Words that have opposite meanings are called **antonyms**.

Antonyms are often used to compare people, animals, or things. Read these sentences.

    That horse is a *tame* animal.
    That zebra is a *wild* animal.

These sentences tell how the horse and the zebra are different. The horse is *tame*, but the zebra is *wild*. *Tame* and *wild* are antonyms.

Dictionaries sometimes give antonyms as well as synonyms for words. Here is a sample dictionary entry for the word *happy*. Notice that synonyms and antonyms for *happy* are listed after the meanings.

> **hap·py 1.** lucky; fortunate **2.** showing a feeling of pleasure **3.** suitable and clever.
> SYNONYMS—glad, joyful, cheerful
> ANTONYMS—sad, sorry

# Exercises  Finding and Using Antonyms

**A.** Find a word on the right that means the opposite of a word on the left. Write both words.

1. dark      go
2. thick     outside
3. empty     light
4. quiet     sad
5. stop      smooth
6. far       full
7. inside    slow
8. rough     near
9. fast      noisy
10. glad     thin

**B.** Read each sentence. Think of a word that means the opposite of each underlined word. Write the word.

1. The baby started crying.
2. Suddenly the lights went off.
3. Wally stood at the top of the hill.
4. The box was very heavy.
5. Margaret has a high voice.
6. Our family woke up late.

**C.** Think of antonyms that complete each pair of sentences. Write the sentences with the antonyms.

1. The engine is the _____ car of the train.
2. The caboose is the _____ car of the train.

3. The boat passed _____ the bridge.
4. The cars drove _____ the bridge.

43

# 6 Finding Clues to Meanings

> The meaning of a word is sometimes given in the sentence. A writer can tell the meaning or give clues to the meaning.

Sometimes you don't have a dictionary handy. Here are some other ways to understand a new word.

**1. Sometimes the sentence where the word is found gives the meaning.**

> The ax made a gash, or long deep cut, in the tree.

The sentence tells you that a *gash* is a long deep cut. *Cut* is a synonym for *gash*.

**2. At other times the writer tells you the meaning of a new word in a separate sentence.**

> Have you ever seen the Milky Way? It is a group of millions of stars.

The second sentence tells what the Milky Way is.

**3. Sometimes a writer gives you only clues to the meaning of a new word.**

> My little brother is a mimic. He often copies other people's actions.

Did you decide that a mimic is a person who copies other people's actions?

## Exercise  Finding Clues to Meanings

Study the following sentences. Find the clue to the meaning of each underlined word. Write the word and the meaning.

1. In the garden are some ladybugs, small red bugs with spotted backs.
2. Dripping water irks me. Flashing lights bother me, too.
3. Some people still live as nomads. They do not settle in one place, but continue to wander.
4. The boat was about to capsize. It was starting to turn over when the Coast Guard arrived.
5. Did you ever see a llama, an animal like a camel without a hump?
6. The earth tremor lasted ten seconds. It shook apart many buildings.
7. Reporters have hectic lives. Their days are often rushed and exciting.
8. Kid is a soft leather. It is made from the skin of goats.
9. Lucia keeps the jewels in a steel vault. She wants to be sure they are in a safe place.
10. Carl paints portraits. Debbie, Walt, and Helen are people whose pictures he has painted.

**Be a word detective.**

# Using English in Spelling

**Homophones** are words that sound alike but are spelled differently. They have different meanings. For example, *rain* and *reign* are homophones. Can a king *rain* for ten years? Of course he can't! The correct word is *reign*. *Reign* means "to rule." *Rain* means "water falling in drops from clouds."

If you are not sure of the spelling of a homophone, use the dictionary. The dictionary will give you the meanings, too. Then you will be sure that you are using the correct word.

### Exercise  Using Homophones Correctly

Choose the correct homophone in parentheses. Write each sentence.

1. Juan used (flour, flower) to make the bread.
2. The rabbit ran into its (hole, whole).
3. I don't (no, know) if Marcy can dance.
4. Did you (hear, here) the siren?
5. Sabrina will (by, buy) some silver paint.
6. I'd like to (meat, meet) the President.
7. The eye doctor asked me to (stare, stair) at the chart.
8. Toby chopped (would, wood) for the fire.
9. Gina's softball team (won, one) every game.
10. The king gets (board, bored) when he stays indoors.

# Chapter 3 Review

**A. Using a Dictionary** Look at this part of a dictionary page. Use it to answer the questions below.

---

**haystack**                                  **heart**

**hay·stack** a large heap of hay piled outdoors.
**haz·ard 1.** danger or something dangerous; [He knew about the *hazards* of icy streets.] **2.** anything on a golf course that makes it harder to play, as a pond or a pit filled with sand.

**haze 1.** thin mist, smoke, or dust in the air that makes it harder to see **2.** the condition of being confused in the mind; daze.
SYNONYMS—mist, fog

---

1. What are the guide words on the page?
2. What example sentence is given?
3. Read the meanings for *hazard*. Write the number that best fits this sentence:
   The golf ball landed in a *hazard*.
4. What is a synonym for *haze*?

**B. Finding Clues to Meanings** Read the following sentences. Find the clue to the meaning of each underlined word. Write the word and its meaning.

1. Eagles have sharp <u>talons</u>, or claws.
2. The old man told us a <u>yarn</u>, a story that is hard to believe.
3. We laughed at the clown's <u>antics</u>. Clowns are good at doing tricks and acting silly.
4. The balloon <u>ascended</u> slowly. As it moved upward, the crowd cheered.

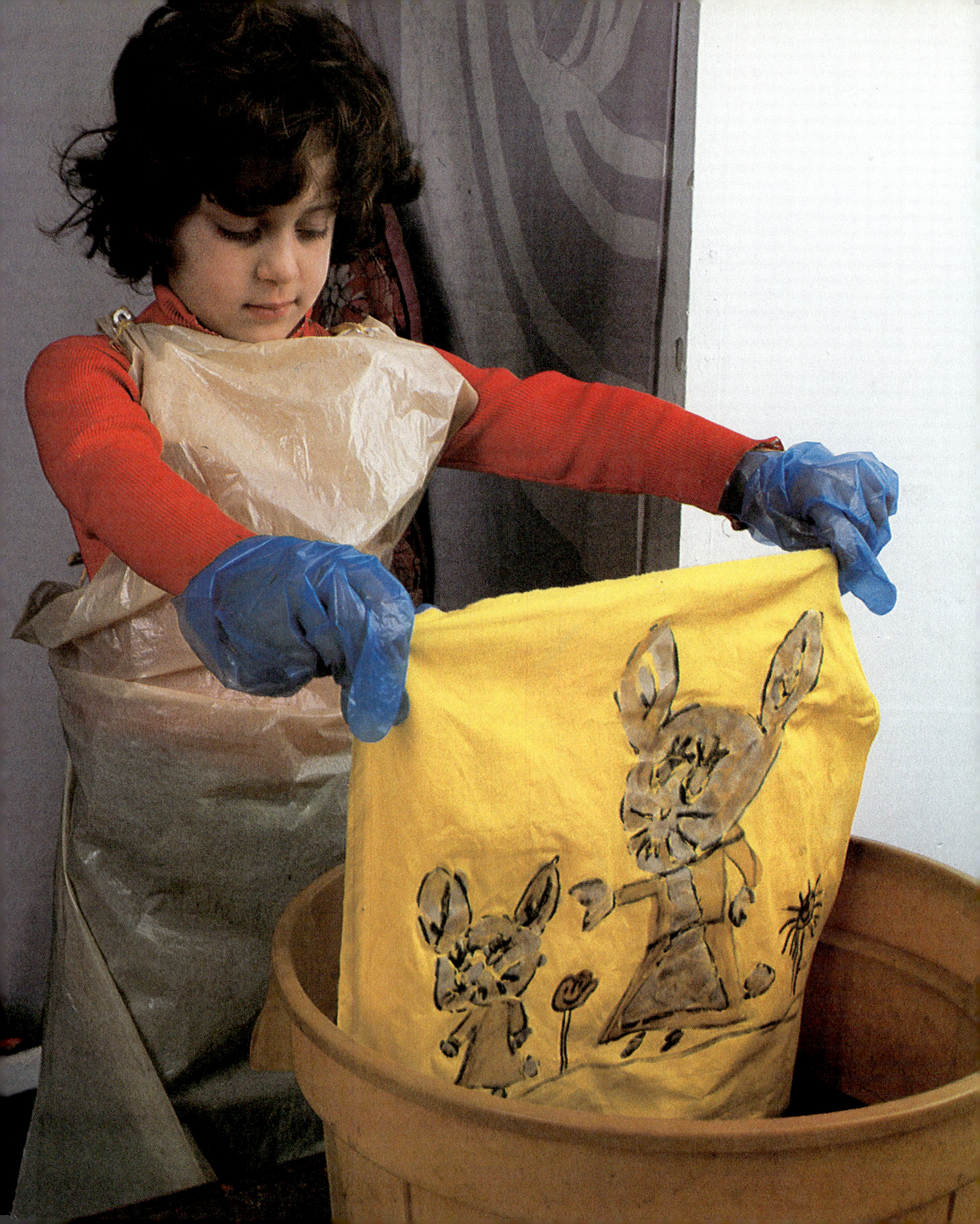

# Chapter 4

# Learning About Sentences

The school band.    Is watching.

These groups of words do not tell us enough. What is the band doing? Who is watching?
Now look at these groups of words.

The school band is playing a tune.
Larry is watching.

Each of these groups of words tells a complete thought. Each one is a sentence.
In this chapter, you will learn about sentences. You will look at the parts of a sentence and at different kinds of sentences. You will learn how to write better sentences.

# 1 What Is a Sentence?

> A **sentence** is a group of words that tells a complete idea.

When you talk or write, you use words. Usually, you put your words together in groups. Some of those groups are **sentences.** Read this group of words.

The deer ran in the forest.

This word group tells a complete idea. It tells about a deer. It tells what the deer did. It is a sentence.

A sentence must have two parts. One part tells **who** or **what** the sentence is about. The second part tells **what happens.** Read the two parts in these sentences.

| who or what | what happens |
|---:|:---|
| The deer | ran in the forest. |
| A squirrel | gathered nuts. |
| Two rabbits | hopped away. |

**Not all groups of words are sentences.** When a group of words does not tell a complete idea, it is not a sentence. Read this group of words.

In the forest.

Who is in the forest? What happened? The group of words does not tell you. It does not give a complete idea. It is not a sentence.

🗝 **Key to Writing and Speaking** When you write or speak, tell complete thoughts. Your readers and listeners will understand what you are telling.

### Exercises   Finding Sentences

**A.** Say each group of words. Decide whether each group of words tells a complete idea. If it does, write **Yes.** If it does not, write **No.**

1. The clown's funny hat.
2. Danny went to the circus.
3. Marcy paints pictures of horses.
4. Slid into home plate.
5. Chris caught a big catfish.
6. In the top row.
7. Watermelons have seeds.
8. The mountain peak.
9. Superman fights crime.
10. Watched a squirrel.

**B.** These groups of words are not sentences. Add words to make each group a sentence. Write the sentences. Make sure that each sentence tells a complete idea.

1. pulled a wagon
2. under my bed
3. loud noises
4. tied a knot
5. magic show
6. in a tree

**C. Writing** Pretend that you are a clown in the circus. You can do many tricks. Write two or more sentences about some tricks you do.

# 2 Kinds of Sentences

> There are four kinds of sentences. They are **statements, questions, commands,** and **exclamations.** Every sentence begins with a capital letter.

Sentences do different jobs. Here are the four kinds of sentences and the job each does. Say the sentences aloud. Let your voice tell the end mark.

**1. A statement is a sentence that tells something. It ends with a period.**

>Billy worked in his garden.
>He grew vegetables.

**2. A question is a sentence that asks something. It ends with a question mark.**

>Are the tomatoes ripe?
>Where are the carrots?

**3. A command is a sentence that tells someone to do something. Usually, a command ends with a period.**

>Please water those flowers.
>Take care of your tools.

**4. An exclamation is a sentence that shows strong feeling. It might show excitement, or anger, or fear. It ends with an exclamation point.**

>Watch out for that bee!
>How fast the weeds grew!

**Exercises** **Understanding the Kinds of Sentences**

**A.** Say each sentence. Decide if it is a **statement, command, question,** or **exclamation.** Write the word that tells what kind of sentence it is.

Example: Keep the gate locked.   command

1. Does your dog do tricks?
2. Karen hit a home run.
3. What a fast boat that is!
4. This toy uses batteries.
5. How sour this apple tastes!
6. Can we ride the smallest pony?
7. Don't touch the wet paint.
8. What a sunburn you have!
9. How much do tickets cost?
10. Ramon likes cowboy stories.

**B.** Say each sentence. Let your voice tell what kind of sentence it is. Write each sentence, using capital letters and correct punctuation.

1. today is my birthday
2. will you come to my party
3. come to my house at noon
4. what a great game this is
5. did you enjoy the party

**C. Writing** You are visiting a farm. Someone calls for help, so you run to look. The gate to the chicken house is open. All the chickens are loose. Write about what you do to help. Try to use all four kinds of sentences.

53

# 3 The Parts of the Sentence

> Every sentence has two parts. The parts are called the **subject** and the **predicate.**

The **subject** of a sentence tells *who* or *what* the sentence is about. A subject may have one word or more than one word. Look at the three sentences below. The subject of each sentence is underlined. Count the words in each subject.

<u>Andrea</u> wins every race.
(who)

<u>Relay races</u> are fun to join.
(what)

<u>Every team member</u> won a prize.
(who)

The **predicate** may tell different things about the subject. It may tell what the subject *does*, what the subject *has*, or what the subject *is*. A predicate may have one or more words.

Andrea <u>races</u>.
(what the subject does)

Andrea <u>has blue running shoes</u>.
(what the subject has)

Andrea <u>is the fastest runner in school</u>.
(what the subject is)

**The Subject in a Command** In a command, the subject is the word *you. You* is understood in the sentence. That means it is not said or written.

> Stay on the path.
> (You) Stay on the path.

## Exercises   Finding Subjects and Predicates

**A.** Write each of the following sentences. Draw one line under the **subject.** Draw two lines under the **predicate.**

1. Henry won a blue ribbon.
2. A huge spaceship landed.
3. Meg and Angie have new bikes.
4. Juan made the final goal.
5. Sandy plays the guitar.
6. Our whole class visited the zoo.
7. The wagon lost a wheel.
8. My mother fixed the broken window.
9. This old bridge is made of wood.
10. Ken took his puppy for a walk.

**B.** Think of a predicate for each subject listed below. Write a sentence using each subject. Then think of a subject for each predicate. Write three more sentences.

| Subjects | Predicates |
| --- | --- |
| the elephant | makes me laugh |
| our team | is always hungry |
| a fire engine | started to swim |

**C. Writing** You are a runner in the Olympics. Write three sentences about the final race. Tell if you win a medal.

# 4 Writing Better Sentences

> A sentence should tell one idea. When you want to tell two ideas, write two sentences.

You have learned that a sentence tells a complete thought or idea. Sometimes you write too many ideas in one sentence. When ideas run together in a sentence, it is called a **run-on sentence.** Here is an example.

Ben likes skating he skates in the park.

Here are the two ideas in the sentence.

1. Ben likes skating
2. he skates in the park

The run-on sentence should be rewritten as two sentences. Each sentence should tell one idea.

Ben likes skating. He skates in the park.

Notice that a period was placed at the end of the first idea. A capital letter was used to begin the second idea. Avoid run-on sentences. Use capital letters and end marks to separate each idea.

 **Key to Writing**  Read your sentences aloud. When you speak, pause at the end of every idea. This will help you decide if you have run two sentences together.

# Exercises   Writing Better Sentences

**A.** Read each group of words. Write **S** if it is a good sentence. Write **R** if it is a run-on sentence.

1. Alex lives on my street do you know him?
2. Mr. Simon read us a story about Mars.
3. Lin collects posters it is her hobby.
4. The train was late I waited an hour.
5. Tyrone went to the park.
6. We went shopping for ice skates.
7. Carla had a party she lives next door.
8. The team got a trophy for winning.
9. Marsha can't swim she has a cold.
10. There is a bike path near my school.

**B.** Look again at the five run-on sentences in Exercise A. Write each one correctly as two complete sentences.

**C. Writing** The following story has three run-on sentences. Rewrite the story, using better sentences. Then add one more sentence to the story.

> Molly was on her way to the library she met Felipe. He had so many books to carry one dropped in a puddle. What a mess it was Molly helped Felipe carry his books.

# Exercises for Mastery Chapter 4

## Learning About Sentences

**A. Finding Sentences** Read each group of words. Decide whether it tells a complete idea. If it does, write **Yes.** If it does not, write **No.**

1. Bears live in the forest.
2. Around the neighborhood.
3. The shark's teeth.
4. Jerry caught a butterfly.
5. A bow and arrow.
6. The monkey jumped on the swing.
7. Climbed the telephone pole.
8. Saw an airplane land.
9. Carmen flew a kite.
10. Landed on the moon.

**B. Understanding the Kinds of Sentences** Write each of these sentences correctly. Use a capital letter at the beginning of each sentence. Use correct end marks.

1. Sheila has a pet gerbil
2. who is making that noise
3. hold this pole for the tent
4. what a big shadow you have
5. did you see the steam engine
6. wolves live in packs
7. feed your brother's goldfish
8. how strange the clouds look
9. Leroy likes to draw cartoons
10. does an owl see better at night

**C. Working with Subjects and Predicates** Write each of the following sentences. Draw one line under the subject of each sentence. Draw two lines under the predicate.

1. Our cat always lands on her feet.
2. The dragon blew fire.
3. A caboose is the last car.
4. Thunderstorms scare me.
5. The fire engine came quickly.
6. My bike has a broken horn.
7. Cleo builds airplane models.
8. Some space stations will have farms.
9. The lion tamer cracked her whip.
10. Sam's new dog sleeps under the porch.

**D. Writing Better Sentences** Read each of these sentences. If it is a good sentence, write **S.** If it is a run-on sentence, rewrite it as two good sentences.

1. Horses like to run they run fast.
2. Nora is always hungry she likes grapes.
3. A new star has been discovered.
4. Matthew dried the dishes yesterday.
5. The music is too loud turn your radio off.
6. Charles has snails in his fish tank.
7. Victor splashed water at Sara.
8. Did you see that race my friend was first.
9. Maria likes the giraffes at the zoo.
10. Don found my hat it was lost.

# Using Grammar in Writing

**A.** A pilot is coming to visit your class. This pilot does dives, loops, and all sorts of stunts with an airplane. Write some things you would like to know about the pilot. Write some questions you would like to ask. Use capital letters and end marks correctly.

**B.** Your cat had kittens. You want to give them away. Write an ad to post in your neighborhood. Tell why you think someone would be lucky to have one of your kittens. Try to use statements, questions, commands, and exclamations in your ad. Draw a picture of the kittens.

**C. Writing Sentences in Math** Write a sentence that answers each of these questions. Be sure your sentence has a subject and a predicate.

1. You bought a dozen oranges. How many oranges do you have?
2. Your change is $1.25 in quarters. How many quarters did you receive?
3. How many sides does a triangle have?
4. A ruler is one foot long. How many inches long is it?
5. The baker had twelve pounds of flour. He used five pounds. How many pounds does he have left?

# Chapter 4 Review

**A. Writing Sentences Correctly** Write each sentence correctly. Then tell what kind of sentence it is.

1. I found a baby kitten
2. pick up your library book
3. did you ever ride a horse
4. we wore silly costumes
5. do not use Dan's crayons
6. what a good mystery story
7. do you like to collect stamps
8. how hot the room is
9. Eva lost her house keys
10. did you hear loud thunder

**B. Finding Subjects and Predicates** For each sentence, underline the subject once and the predicate twice.

1. The basketball bounced off the hoop.
2. Mia and Freddie paddled the canoe.
3. Three bears wandered into the camp.
4. A comet has a sparkling tail.
5. All the rides were free.

**C. Writing Good Sentences** Read each group of words. If it is not a sentence, write **NS**. If it is a run-on sentence, rewrite it as two good sentences.

1. We saw a snake it had a stripe.
2. Nick tagged Sonya she was out.
3. Lion in the cage.
4. My jump rope broke I need a new one.
5. A little red fox.

# Chapter 5

# Writing Paragraphs

Can one color make a rainbow?
Can one page make a book?
Can one sentence tell a story?

It takes many colors to make a rainbow. There are many pages in a book. One sentence cannot tell a story. In writing, we often need more than one sentence to tell an idea. Sometimes we need a group of sentences to tell something. A group of sentences that tells about one idea is called a paragraph.

In this chapter, you will learn to write paragraphs. Writing good paragraphs will help you to share your thoughts and ideas with others.

# 1 Learning About Paragraphs

> A **paragraph** is a group of sentences. Every paragraph has a main idea.

A **paragraph** is a group of sentences. All of the sentences tell about one idea. This idea is called the **main idea** of the paragraph. Read the following paragraph to find the main idea.

> Helena, the Hippopotamus, didn't feel well. She stood all alone in the river and moped. Helena didn't know what to do. She didn't want to eat. She didn't want to swim. She didn't want to play and cool herself in the wet, sticky mud. Poor Helena was very unhappy.
>
> —YUTAKA SUGITA

Helena, the Hippopotamus, felt too sick to do anything. This is the main idea. All of the sentences in the paragraph tell something about this main idea.

Each sentence in the paragraph tells a complete thought. Each sentence begins with a capital letter and ends with a period.

Look at the first line of the paragraph. It is **indented.** That means it begins a few spaces to the right. The first line of a paragraph is always indented.

## Exercises   Understanding Paragraphs

**A.** Read the paragraph. Then choose the main idea below.

> I am a giant. I wake up in the morning and stretch. My hand almost goes through the ceiling. I brush my teeth with a big broom. I eat ten eggs and drink the juice of fifty oranges. Then I take a whole loaf of bread and butter it down the side. I eat it in two gulps because I am a giant.   —IVAN SHERMAN

1. having a giant for a friend
2. the giant's castle
3. what the giant does in the morning

**B.** Write these sentences as a paragraph. Remember to indent the first line. Then write the main idea.

1. There once lived a boy who loved broccoli.
2. He ate broccoli sandwiches.
3. He munched on broccoli chips.
4. He drank big glasses of broccoli juice.
5. He even called himself Broc O'Lee.

**C.** Read this paragraph. Find the sentence that does not tell about the main idea. Write that sentence.

> Jill likes to use the computer. She does math on it. Sometimes she plays games on it. Jill writes stories on the computer. Animal stories are fun to read. Jill wants a job with computers someday.

# 2 The Topic Sentence

> A **topic sentence** gives the main idea of a paragraph.

A paragraph tells one idea. That idea is often given in one sentence, called the **topic sentence.** It is usually the first sentence in a paragraph.

Look at this paragraph. The topic sentence is underlined.

> The crickets and frogs began a musical battle. They wanted to see which could sing the loudest. It was a noisy battle. First the crickets sang out into the night. Then the frogs began. Each one wanted the most silent part of the night for his song. —GABRIELA MISTRAL

The paragraph is about a musical battle between the crickets and frogs. The topic sentence tells this idea. The other sentences tell more about the battle.

Here is another paragraph. The topic sentence is underlined. What is the main idea?

> Charles dreamed about taking pictures with his camera. He took a picture of a cat. He took a picture of a tree. He took a picture of the moon. He took a picture of telephone poles from the window of a speeding car. He took a picture of a rose garden. —MANUS PINKWATER

**Exercise** **Studying Topic Sentences**

Read paragraphs A and B. Then answer these two questions about each paragraph.

1. What is the paragraph about?
2. What is the topic sentence?

**A.** Long ago, African parents taught their children the things they needed to know. The father taught his sons to build the home and to make tools. The mother taught her daughters to grind corn and to cook. She taught both daughters and sons to help care for the younger children.

—MURIEL FEELINGS

**B.** The sea was Maria's only playmate. It talked with Maria. At night it sang her to sleep. It sent its waves along the shore to play games with her. It brought her presents of shells. It gave her the sandy beach all of her own.

—ELIZABETH COATSWORTH

## Now It's Your Turn

You have learned that a paragraph is a group of sentences about one main idea. You have seen that the topic sentence states that main idea.

Now you are going to learn a process for writing a paragraph. This process is a set of steps to follow. These steps will make writing easier for you.

# 3 Learning About Prewriting

> Think about and plan your paragraph before you write. This step is called **prewriting.**

**Prewriting** means getting ready to write. You must think about and plan your paragraph. Before you write, follow these prewriting guides.

**1. Think about a topic.** First, you need to choose a topic to write about. Try brainstorming to find ideas for your paragraph. When you **brainstorm,** you think of as many ideas as you can. You can brainstorm by yourself or with your classmates.

As you brainstorm, make a list of some topic ideas. First, think of some things you know about. For example, do you know how it feels to ride a bike for the first time? Next, use your imagination. Think about an exciting adventure or a new invention. Write all of your ideas on your list. Choose the topic that you would most like to write about.

Remember, your topic should be something you can write about in a paragraph. Here are two lists of topics. The topics on the left side are too big for one paragraph. The other topics are just right.

| pets | my fish tank |
| games | the bike race |
| vacations | sleeping in a tent |
| gardens | planting carrot seeds |

**2. Make notes.** Next, brainstorm for ideas about your topic. Write as many ideas as you can think of. One boy named Phillip chose "my lucky hat" as his topic. Here are the notes Phillip wrote.

has a feather
wear it for tests
wear it to the dentist's
　　office
keep it next to my bed
wore it on the first day
　　of school

**3. Decide on the main idea.** Study your ideas. Decide what the main idea of your paragraph will be.

Phillip studied his ideas. Several of them were about the times he wore his lucky hat. He decided that this would be the main idea of his paragraph.

when I wear my lucky hat

## Exercises  Using Prewriting

**A. Choosing a Topic** Brainstorm with your class to think of topics for a paragraph. Make a list of all the topics that are suggested.

**B. Planning Your Paragraph** Now make a list of topic ideas for your own paragraph. You can use some that your class thought of in Exercise A. You may find others on page 333 of the **Power Handbook.**

　Choose one topic from your list. Make notes about your topic. Then decide what your main idea will be.

# 4 Writing a Draft

> Use your prewriting notes to write a draft of your paragraph.

You are now ready for the second step in the writing process. You are ready to write a draft. A **draft** is the first try at writing a paragraph. It is a way to get your ideas into sentences. It does not have to be perfect.

Start by writing your topic sentence. Then, look at your prewriting notes. Use the notes to write the rest of your sentences. Write a sentence using each of your ideas.

Read Phillip's draft below. First, he wrote his topic sentence. Then, he used his prewriting notes to write sentences about his topic.

I wear my lucky hat on special days. I wore it on the first day of school sometimes on the days I take tests. I keep my hat next to my bed. I wear it to the dentist's office too.

Notice that Phillip used almost all of the ideas from his notes. He turned his ideas into sentences. Phillip left out the idea that his hat has a feather. He decided it was not about the topic.

**Exercises  Writing a Draft**

**A. Building a Paragraph**  Follow these directions. They will guide you in writing a draft.

1. Write this topic sentence on a sheet of paper. Sparky can do three tricks.
2. Study the three pictures. Each picture shows Sparky doing one trick.

3. Write one sentence about each picture.
4. Write all four sentences as a paragraph. Be sure to indent the first line.

**B. Writing Your Draft**  Gather the notes and the main idea that you wrote for part 3 on page 69.

1. Read your notes.
2. Write your topic sentence.
3. Choose three or four things to tell about your topic. Write sentences that tell about the main idea.
4. Write all the sentences as a paragraph.

# 5 Revising a Paragraph

> Read your paragraph and change it to make it better. This step is called **revising.**

You have written a paragraph. However, it is not finished. Now you must try to make your paragraph better. Changing your writing to make it better is called **revising,** or editing.

Here are questions, or guides, that will help you.

**Guides for Revising a Paragraph**

1. Is every word group in the paragraph a sentence?
2. Do all the sentences tell about the same topic? Should any be taken out?
3. Is the paragraph easy to understand? Should anything be added?

When Phillip revised his paragraph, he marked the changes on his paper. As you study his draft, notice the changes. Try to decide why he made them.

I wear my lucky hat on special days. I wore it on the first day of school. Sometimes I wear it on the days I take tests. ~~I keep my hat next to my bed.~~ I wear my lucky hat to the dentist's office too.

**1.** Phillip decided that his second sentence was not clear or correct. He changed it into two sentences.

**2.** Phillip also realized that the sentence about where he kept his hat did not really tell about the topic. He drew a line through the words that did not belong.

**3.** Phillip revised his last sentence by adding words. Notice how he marked the changes.

Here are the marks you can use for revising your writing.

### Marks for Revising Your Writing

≡ Capitalize a letter.

⊙ Put in a period.

∧ Add words.

— Take out words.

/ Change a capital letter to lowercase.

↗ Add a comma.

¶ Begin a new paragraph.

## Exercise  Revising Your Paragraph

Read the draft you wrote for part 4. Try to make it better. Follow the Guides for Revising a Paragraph on page 72. Mark the changes on your paragraph.

# 6 Finishing and Sharing a Paragraph

> Proofread your paragraph. Then make a final copy to share with others.

You have written a paragraph. You have revised your paragraph by changing or adding words and sentences. Now you are ready for the final steps of the process of writing.

**Proofread your paragraph.** Look for mistakes in capital letters, punctuation, and spelling. This is called **proofreading.** You can use the marks on page 73 to mark corrections. Here are some guides to help you proofread your paragraph.

### Guides for Proofreading a Paragraph

1. Is the first line indented?
2. Does every sentence begin with a capital letter?
3. Does every proper noun begin with a capital letter?
4. Does every sentence have the correct end mark?
5. Are all of the words spelled correctly?

**Make a final copy.** Writing is a way of sharing ideas with others. Your writing should be clear enough for someone else to read. When you make your final copy, be sure you have made all of your changes. Use your best handwriting.

Here is the final copy of Phillip's paragraph.

> I wear my lucky hat on special days. I wore it on the first day of school. Sometimes I wear it on the days I take tests. I wear my lucky hat to the dentist's office too.

You have learned how to write good paragraphs. Remember these steps.

**Steps for Writing a Paragraph**

1. Think about a topic.
2. Write notes about your topic.
3. Write a topic sentence.
4. Use your notes to write sentences. This is your draft.
5. Read your draft carefully. Revise it. Mark changes that will make it a clearer and better paragraph.
6. Proofread for mistakes in the paragraph. Mark your corrections.
7. Make a clean copy of your paragraph. Make the changes and corrections that you marked on the draft. Write neatly.

## Exercise   Finishing and Sharing Your Paragraph

Look for mistakes in your paragraph. Follow the Guides for Proofreading a Paragraph on page 74. Mark all of the corrections on your paper.

Make a clean copy of your paragraph. Then, decide how you would like to share your writing. You might read it aloud or put it on the bulletin board.

# Speaking and Listening

### Giving a Talk

There are several ways to share ideas. One way is by giving a talk. You learned how to plan a written paragraph. You can plan a talk the same way.

Choose your topic. Decide what you are going to tell about it. Get ready to give your talk. Use notes if you need them. Speak clearly in a pleasant voice.

### Exercise   Telling About a Hobby

Do you like to collect stamps or coins? Do you like a certain sport? Maybe drawing or painting is something you like to do. If you like an activity, you can call it a **hobby.**

Think about your hobby. Plan a talk about it. Bring in samples or pictures to share with your audience.

Remember to be a good listener when other people are talking. Listening is a way of sharing, too.

# Creative Writing

**A.** Crash! Boom! Your spaceship has landed on an unknown planet. Give your planet a name. Write a paragraph that tells what you see. Use the name of the planet in your topic sentence. Tell about the land, the people (if there are any), and anything else you see on the planet.

**B.** "It was so hot, we fried eggs on the sidewalk." This idea may be silly, but it is fun to write about. Choose one of the ideas below or make up your own. Think of several things that would happen if it were very hot, or cold, or windy. Write a paragraph that starts with that sentence. Use your imagination.

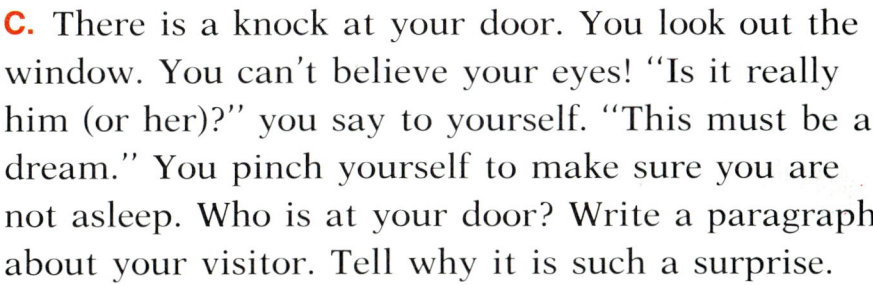

It was so hot. . .
It was so cold. . .
It was so windy. . .
It was so foggy. . .
It was so rainy. . .

**C.** There is a knock at your door. You look out the window. You can't believe your eyes! "Is it really him (or her)?" you say to yourself. "This must be a dream." You pinch yourself to make sure you are not asleep. Who is at your door? Write a paragraph about your visitor. Tell why it is such a surprise.

## Using English in Science

Scientists learn by observing. A scientist does an experiment. He or she studies what happens. Then the scientist writes about it. You can write about a science experiment too. Use what you have learned about writing good paragraphs.

**Exercise** **Writing About a Science Experiment**

Abby wanted to find out how plants get water and food. Read the five steps of her experiment.

1. First, Abby added red food coloring to a glass of water.
2. Then, she cut a small piece off the bottom of a stalk of celery.
3. She placed the stalk in the red water.
4. She looked at the celery every hour. After four hours, Abby saw red lines going up the stalk. The leaves were turning red, too.
5. She cut another piece off the bottom. She saw red dots on it. Each dot was the end of a tube that went up the stalk. They were the red lines Abby saw.

What did Abby find out from her experiment? Write a paragraph to tell how plants get water and food. Then try the experiment yourself.

# Chapter 5 Review

**A. Understanding Paragraphs** Read this paragraph. Write the sentence that does not belong.

> My friend Alexis went on a trip to Arizona. She brought back some Indian beads and arrowheads. She made a poster of arrowheads and beads. She makes me laugh a lot. She hung it in her room.

**B. Finding the Topic Sentence** Read this paragraph. Answer the questions that follow.

> Mr. Sito was very, very old. He was much, much older than I am. He was much older than my mother and father. He was much older than all my aunts and uncles. He was even a little bit older than the white-haired bakery-man down the block.
>
> —JOAN FASSLER

1. What is the main idea?
2. What is the topic sentence of the paragraph?

**C. Understanding Proofreading Marks** Read this paragraph. Look at the corrections that are marked. Rewrite the paragraph with the changes.

> I met a cowboy once. His name was Jake. He told me about wild horses. How to catch them. And to rope them. And to tame them. He wore chaps. It was fun to meet jake.

# Cumulative Review

Unit 1

## Composition

**Writing a Paragraph** Write a paragraph about something you wish for. Your topic sentence should tell what your wish is. The rest of the sentences should tell what would happen if you get your wish.

## Grammar

**A. Sentences** Read each group of words. If it is not a sentence, write **NS.** If it is a sentence, rewrite it correctly.

1. can you snap your fingers
2. take off the blindfold
3. the barn is on fire
4. the giant redwood trees
5. loren drew a map for us
6. who broke the piñata
7. played a video game
8. please save me a seat
9. jimena takes karate lessons
10. what big muscles you have

**B. Parts of a Sentence** Write each sentence. Underline the subject once and the predicate twice.

1. Kangaroos come from Australia.
2. The old fence was falling apart.
3. Anita and Terry made paper fans.
4. The campers raise the flag every morning.
5. My mom and dad caught eight fish.

## Related Skills

**A. Building New Words** Add a prefix or suffix to each word below to build a new word.

    work    build    seat    button    score

**B. Using the Dictionary** Look at this part of a dictionary page. Use it to answer the questions below.

---

**bike**                                                                      **blizzard**

**bike 1.** bicycle **2.** motorcycle.

**bind 1.** to tie together **2.** to bandage **3.** to fasten the pages of a book together.
SYNONYMS: tie, fasten
ANTONYM: separate

**blintz** [Russian] a thin pancake rolled with a filling of cheese or fruit.

**blip 1.** an image on a screen **2.** a very quick, sharp sound.

---

1. What are the guide words on the page?
2. Which meaning for *bind* best fits this sentence?
    Dr. Samuels is going to *bind* your sprained ankle.
3. Which entry word from the sample page is an echoic word? Which entry word is a borrowed word?
4. What is the meaning of *rebind*?
5. What word means the opposite of the word *bind*?

# UNIT 2

Chapter 6 **Learning About Nouns**
Chapter 7 **Learning About Pronouns**
Chapter 8 **Telling a Story**
Chapter 9 **Learning About Verbs**
Chapter 10 **Writing a Story**

## Gathering Words into Ideas

In Unit 2, you will begin to learn about some of the different groups of words in our language. You will also study how to tell and write a story.

You will learn how nouns, pronouns, and verbs are used. You will see these words at work in stories. You will discover how to keep your listener's attention when you tell or write a story yourself.

Your new skills will help you in all of your speaking and writing. They will also help you to tell about events that happened long ago in history. You can use these skills to describe what you discover in science.

What you learn will also help you share your own special ideas and stories with others. You will be able to put your dreams into words and bring them to life.

# DREAM DUST

Gather out of star-dust
    Earth-dust,
    Cloud-dust,
    Storm-dust,
And splinters of hail,
One handful of dream-dust
    Not for sale.

—LANGSTON HUGHES

**Chapter 6**

# Learning About Nouns

You are a student. You are at school. You are reading a book.

*Student* is a word that names you. *School* is a word that names where you are. *Book* names the thing you are reading. *Student, school*, and *book* are all nouns. Nouns are the words that name persons, places, and things.

In this chapter, you will learn about the kinds of nouns. You will learn how to write special names. You will also learn how nouns change their forms. As you learn how to use nouns correctly, your writing will become better and clearer.

# 1 What Are Nouns?

> A **noun** is a word that names a person, a place, or a thing.

Everything you see has a word that names it. These names are nouns. **Nouns** are the words for persons, places, or things. Here are some nouns that name persons, places, or things.

**Persons**  student, girl, dentist
**Places**   school, home, town
**Things**   book, apple, hat

The nouns above name someone or something you can see. Other nouns name things you cannot see. They may be things you hear or feel. They may be ideas. These nouns name things you cannot see.

voices   wind   love   friendship

A noun can be used as the subject of a sentence.

My <u>bicycle</u> is blue.   The <u>boy</u> ran.

A noun can also be used in the predicate of a sentence.

I rode the <u>bus</u>.   She met her <u>friends</u>.

🔑 **Key to Writing and Speaking:** Nouns help to make your writing and speaking clear. Choose nouns that are as exact as possible. Use the word *grapes* instead of *fruit*. Say *daisy* instead of *flower*.

## Exercises   Finding Nouns

**A.** Each of the following sentences has two or more nouns. Write the sentences. Underline the nouns.

1. Rabbits live in my yard.
2. This store sells boots and shoes.
3. Your dog barked at the squirrel.
4. The wind blew down the sign.
5. My friend made a wish on a star.
6. Two tiny cars raced on the track.
7. Some airplanes land on water.
8. Our cousins live on a ranch.
9. That driver found a dime and a quarter.
10. The monkey ate nuts, raisins, and a banana.

**B.** On your paper, make lists of nouns according to these directions.

1. Names of four vegetables
2. Names of four kinds of animals
3. Names of four things with wheels
4. Names of four pieces of furniture

**C. Writing** Imagine that you have a secret room. Write about it. Use nouns to tell what is in the room. Tell how it feels to be there.

## 2 Common Nouns and Proper Nouns

> A **common noun** is a general name for persons, places, or things. A **proper noun** names a particular person, place, or thing. Begin every important word of a proper noun with a capital letter.

The word *woman* stands for any woman. The word *city* stands for any city. *City* and *woman* are both common nouns. **Common nouns** are general names for persons, places, or things.

Another kind of noun names a particular person, place, or thing. *Thomas Baker* is the name of a particular person. *Boston* is the name of a particular city. *Thomas Baker* and *Boston* are proper nouns. **Proper nouns** begin with capital letters.

| Common Noun | Proper Noun |
|---|---|
| teacher | Mr. Gomez |
| pet | Queenie |
| day | Monday |
| month | November |
| holiday | Veteran's Day |

Some proper nouns have more than one word. Do not use capital letters for little words like *in, of,* or *the.* Write "the Statue of Liberty."

**Exercises** **Finding Common Nouns and Proper Nouns**

**A.** Write each of the following nouns. Remember to use capital letters for proper nouns.

1. mars
2. planet
3. school
4. florida
5. africa
6. president adams
7. dr. hansen
8. dentist
9. january
10. rebecca

**B.** Write these headings on your paper: **Common Nouns, Proper Nouns.** Find a common noun and a proper noun in each sentence. Write each noun under the correct heading.

1. Ben Franklin worked as a printer.
2. California is along the ocean.
3. Pumpkins are carved on Halloween.
4. Steamboats sail on the Mississippi River.
5. His tribe is the Navaho.
6. Switzerland has many mountains.
7. Cross the bridge on Lake Street.
8. The *Nautilus* is a submarine.
9. Heidi collects old magazines.
10. Our class visited the Washington Monument recently.

**C. Writing** You have been chosen to show your city to a famous person. Tell who the famous person is. Write about the places you will take the person to see. Use common nouns and proper nouns.

# 3 Singular Nouns and Plural Nouns

> A **singular noun** names one person, place, or thing. A **plural noun** names more than one person, place, or thing.

The noun *apple* names one thing. It is a **singular noun.** The noun *apples* names more than one thing. *Apples* is a **plural noun.**

Most nouns change their form to show when they are plural. Here are the most common ways to change singular nouns to plural nouns:

1. **Add -s to most singular nouns.**

   fruit*s*   vegetable*s*   meat*s*   food*s*

2. **When the singular noun ends in s, sh, ch, or x, add -es.**

   **s**  bus*es*          **ch**  sandwich*es*
   **sh** bush*es*         **x**   fox*es*

3. **When the singular noun ends in a consonant and y, change the y to i and add -es.**

   penny—penn*ies*   hobby—hobb*ies*   fly—fl*ies*

4. **Some singular nouns form their plurals in special ways.**

   man—men       woman—women      tooth—teeth
   foot—feet     child—children   mouse—mice

90

**Exercises**  **Forming Plural Nouns**

**A.** Write the following nouns. After each singular noun, write **s.** After each plural noun, write **pl.**

1. feet
2. cookies
3. story
4. branches
5. flower
6. vase
7. mice
8. donkey
9. boxes
10. eyes
11. cities
12. dress
13. tables
14. ear
15. men

**B.** Write the following singular nouns. After each noun, write the plural of that noun. Be able to tell which rule on page 90 helped you.

1. pony
2. tax
3. woman
4. lunch
5. camel
6. brush
7. child
8. party
9. tooth
10. berry

**C. Writing** Ellen's cat had kittens. Ellen began to write about things she would need for two pets. She wrote the following:

I need two bowls, two _____

Finish Ellen's note. Write all the things that you think she will need for the pets.

## 4 Making Nouns Show Possession

> A **possessive noun** shows ownership.

You have learned how to write common nouns and proper nouns. You know how to change the form of a singular noun to make it a plural noun.

A noun may also be written to show that a person or an animal owns something. When a noun shows ownership, it is called a **possessive noun**. Look at these pairs of words.

Ms. Regan's keys    Dad's car    dog's collar

In each pair, the first noun is a possessive noun. The second noun tells what belongs to that person or animal. The mark used is an **apostrophe** (').

Here are the ways to make nouns show possession.

**1. To make a singular noun show possession, add an apostrophe and an *s*.**

Jason's bike    the teacher's desk

**2. If a plural noun ends in *s*, add only an apostrophe to show possession.**

the girls' bikes    the teachers' desks

**3. If a plural noun does not end in *s*, add an apostrophe and an *s* to show possession.**

the children's game    the mice's nest

**Exercises    Making Nouns Show Possession**

**A.** Here are two lists of nouns. Write the possessive form of each noun in the first list. Then match it with a noun from the second list. Your answers can be silly.

Example: elephant's trunk

List 1
bee
brother
alligator
clowns
grandmother

List 2
costumes
cage
smile
knees
wings

**B.** Write each sentence. Make each underlined noun a possessive noun. The noun should show ownership.

1. David baby sister shakes hands.
2. The blackbirds cries are loud.
3. My grandfather house is nearby.
4. The mice nest is under the porch.
5. Barbara joined the girls game.
6. We listened to Ms. Chin directions.
7. The winners prizes are valuable.
8. Sarah climbed into the engineer seat.
9. The dentist cleaned Hector teeth.
10. Both cats tails are black.

**C. Writing** You are going to live in a space station. You want to take something along that belongs to each person in your family. For example, you might take your mother's pen. Make a list of things you would take. Use possessive nouns to show ownership.

# Exercises for Mastery  Chapter 6
## Learning About Nouns

**A. Finding Nouns** Write the following sentences. Underline every noun.

1. The soup was made with vegetables.
2. Miguel collects colorful rocks.
3. The breeze tickles my nose.
4. My dog can catch a newspaper.
5. A whale makes a strange sound.
6. The cereal is on the top shelf.
7. Carol draws cartoons about monkeys.
8. The magazine has a story by Ray Bradbury.
9. Alex and his family had a picnic.
10. Raccoons sometimes sleep in hollow logs.

**B. Finding Common Nouns and Proper Nouns** Write these headings on your paper: **Common Nouns, Proper Nouns.** Find common nouns and proper nouns in these sentences. Write each noun under the correct heading.

1. Marie Curie was a famous scientist.
2. The Photography Club meets after school.
3. The spaceship circled Jupiter.
4. Ulysses S. Grant was a general.
5. The circus is coming to Chicago in October.
6. Roanoke is a city in the United States.
7. The New York Yankees will play our team.
8. Jeff read a book by Dr. Seuss.
9. Marta will live in Spain next summer.
10. The new store is on Noble Road.

**C. Forming Plural Nouns** Write the following singular nouns. After each noun, write the plural form of that noun. You may need to look at the rules on page 90.

1. dog
2. home
3. dish
4. fairy
5. ax
6. kitten
7. foot
8. box
9. monster
10. city
11. table
12. porch
13. man
14. mouse
15. story

**D. Making Nouns Show Possession** Write each sentence. Change the underlined noun to a possessive noun. You will have to add an apostrophe and an **s** to some of the nouns. To others, you will add only an apostrophe.

Example: Barry jacket
Barry's jacket

1. Your scissors are on Kate desk.
2. Charlie Brown filled Snoopy dish.
3. The women boots have rubber heels.
4. Those leaves hid the bird nest.
5. Raoul brushed the dog fur.
6. The clowns cars are tiny.
7. The children feet are covered with sand.
8. Nora sister joined the tumbling team.
9. The Eskimo followed a bear tracks.
10. The nurses uniforms are clean and white.

# Using Grammar in Writing

**A.** Write the name of your favorite holiday. Then think of names for a girl, a boy, a city, an animal, and a food that begin with the same letter. Use the names to write a silly story. Here is an example using words that start with the letter *P*.

> It was Presidents' Day. Pat and Pam stayed home in Pittsburgh. They fed their parrot some peanuts.

**B.** Become familiar with the **Word Bank for Writers** that begins on page 341. You will find words there to use in your writing. Choose a group of words, such as *animals* or *buildings and places*. Write one paragraph using words in that group. Draw a picture that tells about your paragraph.

**C. Using Nouns in Science** Your home may be called a *house* or an *apartment*. Some animals have special names for their homes. For example, a bear's home is called a *den*. Think of three animals or insects. Find out what their homes are called. You may use a science book or encyclopedia. Write sentences telling the names of the animals and their homes.

# Chapter 6 Review

**A. Finding Common Nouns and Proper Nouns** Write these two headings on your paper: **Common Nouns, Proper Nouns.** Find all the nouns in these sentences. Write each noun under the correct heading.

1. The parrot belongs to Mrs. Ferguson.
2. Our family camped at Yellowstone National Park.
3. The parade was on Fifth Avenue.
4. Seth pulled the wagon up the hill.
5. Texas has a center for astronauts.
6. Fran went to a play at the Crown Theater.
7. Hal got a scrapbook for his birthday.
8. Camels live on the desert in Africa.
9. The Reptile Museum has models of dinosaurs.
10. Jessica saw how money was printed in Washington, D.C.

**B. Forming Plural Nouns That Show Possession**
Change each underlined noun to a plural noun. Make it show possession. Write the new pairs of words.

Example: <u>doctor</u> offices
doctors' offices

1. <u>pilot</u> cabins
2. <u>woman</u> jobs
3. <u>officer</u> hats
4. <u>cub</u> paws
5. <u>fly</u> wings
6. <u>fox</u> tails
7. <u>child</u> zoo
8. <u>puppy</u> ears
9. <u>mouse</u> cage
10. <u>pony</u> reins

# Chapter 7

# Learning About Pronouns

Read these two paragraphs.

> John has a new football. John bought the football last week. John and a friend play with the football after school.

> John has a new football. He bought it last week. He and a friend play with it after school.

In the first paragraph, how many times is *John* used? How many times is *football* used? Are these words repeated too many times?

In the second paragraph, *he* and *it* are used instead of *John* and *football*. *He* and *it* are examples of pronouns. Pronouns are words used in place of nouns.

In this chapter, you will learn about pronouns. You will learn about the correct ways to use them.

# 1  What Are Pronouns?

> A **pronoun** is a word that stands for a noun.

Find the nouns in this sentence.

Betsy found a shell.

Did you find *Betsy* and *shell*? *Betsy* is a proper noun. It names a person. *Shell* is a common noun. It names a thing. Here is another way to write this sentence.

She found it.

The word *she* stands for *Betsy*. The word *it* is used in place of *shell*. The words *she* and *it* are pronouns. A **pronoun** is a word that stands for a noun.

In the chapter about nouns, you learned that a noun can be singular or plural. A pronoun can also be singular or plural. The chart below shows the forms of some important pronouns.

| Singular | Plural | |
|---|---|---|
| I, me | we, us | Use these pronouns to talk about yourself. |
| you | you | Use these pronouns to talk about people you are speaking to. |
| he, him she, her it | they, them | Use these pronouns to talk about other persons or things. |

**Exercises**   **Finding Pronouns**

**A.** Write the following sentences. Underline the pronouns.

1. I told her about the lighthouse.
2. Liz invited Cary and me to the circus.
3. We rode on a tractor at Uncle Ted's farm.
4. Will you tell me a ghost story?
5. He made a touchdown at the last minute.
6. The magician fooled them with scarves.
7. Can you find the North Star?
8. She is Tammy's best friend.
9. The scream made us shiver.
10. Martin traded baseball cards with him.

**B.** Find every pronoun in the following sentences. Write each pronoun. Then write the noun or nouns the pronoun stands for.

1. Vera was late. Maria waited for her.
2. Bob lost a dime. He looked for it.
3. Della picked strawberries. She likes them.
4. The camera broke. Dad fixed it.
5. Kit and Beth are friends. They swim together.
6. The class went on a trip. We went to the zoo.
7. The telephone rang, and Joe answered it.
8. Steve caught two frogs. Later he freed them.
9. Patty, do you have the bicycle pump?
10. Clams have shells. They are protected by them.

**C. Writing** You own a talking robot. The robot does whatever you tell it to do. Write about the robot. Use the pronouns *I, me, it,* and *you.*

## 2 Using Pronouns as Subjects

> Only these pronouns may be used as subjects of sentences. **I we you he she it they**

A noun may be used in any place in a sentence. However, only these pronouns may be used as the subject of a sentence: *I, you, we, they, he, she, it.*

I play checkers often.
You are a good player.
We can take turns.
They enjoyed playing.
He is learning the game.
She won that time.
It is not a hard game.

Some subjects have two parts. One or both parts may be pronouns.

Meg and you go first.   He and I go next.

When one part of the subject is a pronoun, you need to choose the correct pronoun.

Larry and (me, I) played two games today.

To choose, take the subject apart. Leave out *Larry.* Then try each pronoun separately. You can tell that the pronoun *I* is the correct one.

Me played two games today.
I played two games today.

🔑 **Key to Writing and Speaking** Whenever you name yourself and another person, name yourself last. For example, if you are part of the subject of the sentence, say: *Karen and I are good players too.*

### Exercises  Using Pronouns as Subjects

**A.** Choose the correct pronoun in each sentence. Write the pronouns.

1. (He, Him) watched the puppet show.
2. (She, Her) is working a puzzle.
3. Mom and (I, me) played the piano.
4. Lily and (them, they) visited Georgia.
5. (We, Us) planned a carnival.
6. Scott and (him, he) hunted for worms.
7. Dad and (me, I) jogged to the beach.
8. (They, Them) searched for their dog.
9. (Her, She) and Frank missed the parade.
10. Kumi and (he, him) put up the flag.

**B.** In each sentence below, the subject is a noun. Change the subject to a pronoun. Write your new sentence.

1. The movie had a funny ending.
2. Mrs. Johnson drove us to the ice rink.
3. Thomas Jefferson was a clever man.
4. The girls built a model airplane.
5. My class made a windmill.

**C. Writing** Tell about a person in your family. Write a paragraph about something you like to do together. Use the pronouns *he, she, we,* and *I* as subjects in some sentences.

# 3 Pronouns in Other Parts of the Sentence

> The pronouns **me, us, him, her,** and **them** may not be used as subjects. They may be used in other parts of a sentence.
>
> The pronouns **it** and **you** may be used anywhere in a sentence.

The following sentences show some correct ways to use *me, us, him, her,* and *them.*

Look at me.
Roberto gave the ball to us.
The letter for him is on the table.
Grandmother asked her a question.
Laura called them to dinner.

*It* and *you* may be used anywhere in a sentence.

It landed on the roof.
Dori caught it.
You hit the ball.
I'm glad to see you.

**🗝 Key to Writing**  Be sure your readers can figure out what noun your pronoun stands for. Suppose you write, "My cat and my dad both have whiskers. He shaves his." It would be clearer to write, "My dad shaves his."

104

**Exercises** **Using Pronouns in Other Parts of the Sentence**

**A.** Write the correct pronoun in each sentence.

1. Heather hit the ball to (he, him).
2. The costume is too big for (her, she).
3. The seals splashed water on (they, them).
4. The pitcher signed the baseball for (me, I).
5. Manuel let (we, us) use his computer.
6. Fiona made a soap carving for (him, he).
7. Dad took (she, her) to the aquarium.
8. Penny asked (we, us) a riddle.
9. Lin played space patrol with (I, me).
10. The puppies jumped on (them, they).

**B.** Use a pronoun in place of the underlined word or words. Write your new sentence.

1. Will your hamster eat <u>the lettuce</u>?
2. Jay gave <u>his sister</u> a clown mask.
3. The captain showed <u>our class</u> the compass.
4. Mom made a bulletin board for <u>Daryl</u>.
5. The engineer waved to <u>Sue and me</u>.
6. I can see <u>the birdhouse</u> from my window.
7. Wind up the clock for <u>Juanita</u>.
8. Anita read a poem to <u>Val and Roman</u>.
9. Do the magic trick for <u>Neil</u>.
10. The trainer let <u>Raj and Leah</u> pet the cub.

**C. Writing** Write about a sports hero. Use pronouns instead of the hero's name. Trade papers with a friend. See if you can guess your friend's sports hero.

## 4 Possessive Pronouns

> A pronoun that shows ownership is a **possessive pronoun**.

You have learned that nouns can show ownership. They do this by adding an apostrophe, or an apostrophe and an *s*.

*Mother's* job    the *boys'* gloves

Pronouns can show ownership too. Unlike nouns, they do not add an apostrophe and *s*. Instead, there are special pronouns, called **possessive pronouns**, that show ownership.

*her* job    *their* gloves

In the examples above, the pronouns *her* and *their* are possessive pronouns. They are used with nouns to show ownership. There are also possessive pronouns that are used alone. Here are examples of both kinds of possessive pronouns.

| Used with Nouns | Used Alone |
|---|---|
| *Our* bus is yellow. | The yellow bus is *ours*. |
| *Her* coat was missing. | The missing coat was *hers*. |
| *My* pencil is sharp. | The sharp pencil is *mine*. |

Study the chart on the following page. It shows all the possessive pronouns.

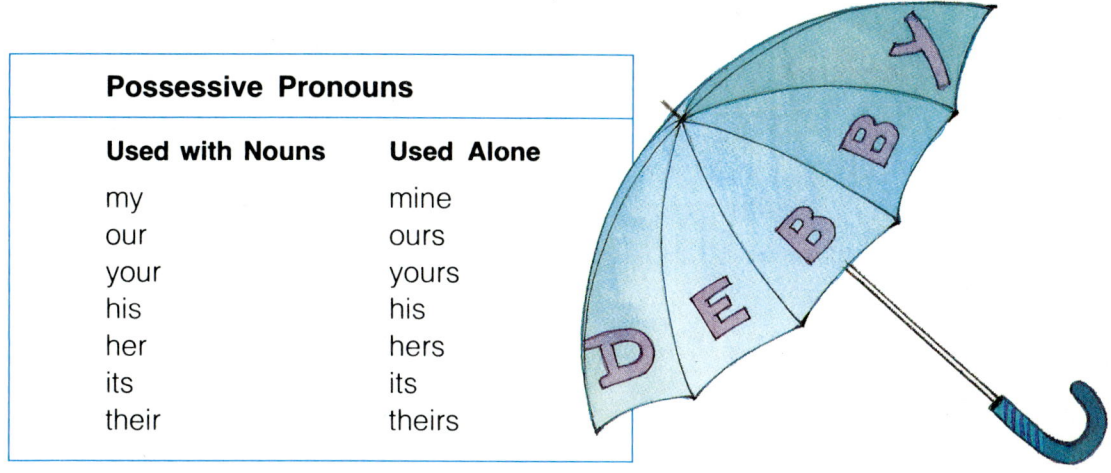

| Possessive Pronouns | |
|---|---|
| **Used with Nouns** | **Used Alone** |
| my | mine |
| our | ours |
| your | yours |
| his | his |
| her | hers |
| its | its |
| their | theirs |

## Exercises  Using Possessive Pronouns

**A.** Choose the correct pronoun from those in parentheses. Write the pronouns.

1. The elephants raised (their, theirs) trunks.
2. Miss Anderson is (hers, her) coach.
3. The blue suitcase is (our, ours).
4. That chess set is (your, yours).
5. Joseph's dog chased (mine, my) cat.

**B.** Use a possessive pronoun in place of the underlined word or words. Write your new sentence.

1. That camera is <u>my camera</u>.
2. Ramsey is <u>Rochelle's</u> parrot.
3. Is this <u>Jeff's</u> soccer ball?
4. The keys are <u>May's and Ted's</u>.
5. Debby, take <u>Debby's</u> umbrella today.

**C. Writing** Your pet frog got out of its box. Write about how your neighbor found it. Use possessive pronouns.

# 5 Using *Its*, *It's*, *Their*, *There*, and *They're*

> Some pronouns sound like other words. Be careful when you use **its** and **it's**. Also be careful when you use **their**, **there**, and **they're**.

## *Its* and *It's*

The possessive pronoun **its** looks very much like the word **it's**. *It's* has an apostrophe to show that something is missing. *It's* stands for *it is* or *it has*.

The TV set is old. *It's* broken. (It is)
We are all tired. *It's* been a long day. (It has)

The possessive pronoun *its* does not have an apostrophe. Its means "belonging to it."

The dog hurt its paw. (The paw belongs to it.)

## *Their*, *There*, and *They're*

The possessive pronoun **their** sounds like the words **there** and **they're**. The three words have different spellings and different meanings.

*Their* means "belonging to them."
*There* means "at that place."
*They're* is a contraction for "they are."

The team wore *their* jackets.
My class was *there* to cheer.
*They're* going to win the game.

108

**Exercises** Using *Its, It's, Their, There,* and *They're* **Correctly**

**A.** Choose the correct word from the parentheses.

1. (It's, Its) muddy in the field.
2. The twins lost (there, their, they're) gloves.
3. That robin has a worm in (it's, its) beak.
4. (There, Their, They're) taking a canoe ride.
5. Did the dog find (it's, its) bone?
6. We left our library books (they're, there, their).
7. (It's, Its) become too dark to play outside.
8. The girls flew (there, their, they're) kites.
9. My cat caught (it's, its) tail in the door.
10. (There, Their, They're) uncle is a firefighter.

**B.** In these sentences, **its, it's, their, there,** and **they're** may be used incorrectly. Write the sentences correctly.

1. Their rabbit got out of it's cage.
2. There playing horseshoes in their yard.
3. It's too late to call there house.
4. They're cat is licking its paws.
5. Its raining, so their picnic was called off.
6. Their watching the elephant wash it's back.
7. Sonya and Ken hang there pictures their.
8. A sparrow made it's nest in there tree.
9. They're getting a tent for there trip.
10. Its important to check their spacesuits.

**C. Writing** You want to surprise your parents with a gift. Write a paragraph telling about the gift. Tell how you think they will like it. Use *its, it's, there, their,* and *they're*.

# Exercises for Mastery

Chapter 7

## Learning About Pronouns

**A. Finding Pronouns** Write every pronoun used in these sentences. After each pronoun, write the noun or nouns it stands for. Some sentences have more than one pronoun.

1. A deer crossed the road. It looked scared.
2. Sally's skates hurt. They are small for her.
3. Kevin likes to dance. He danced today.
4. Tabby loves tuna. She eats it every day.
5. Franco has the tools. He is using them.
6. The moon has craters. They look like big holes.
7. Mark met an astronaut. He talked to her.
8. Gina entered a contest. She won it.
9. Whales live in water, but they are not fish.
10. Clare dunked for the apple. She got it.

**B. Using Pronouns** Write the following sentences. Choose the correct pronoun.

1. (She, Her) wants a book about stars.
2. The juggler did a trick for (we, us).
3. A dolphin swam past (I, me).
4. (Them, They) sold lemonade.
5. The puzzle was easy for (her, she) and him.
6. (We, Us) raced our toy cars.
7. Dad took pictures of Theresa and (I, me).
8. Kitty and (him, he) have pen pals in Iowa.
9. Vadim and (I, me) rowed the boat.
10. The guide put up the tent for (they, them).

**C. Using Possessive Pronouns** Use a possessive pronoun in place of the underlined word or words. Write your new sentences.

1. Is this flashlight <u>your flashlight</u>?
2. <u>Jane's</u> prize is a blue ribbon.
3. That truck is <u>Andrew's toy</u>.
4. That pair of ballet shoes is <u>Paula's</u>.
5. This typewriter is <u>yours and mine</u>.
6. The spider spun <u>the spider's</u> web.
7. Mr. Stone opened <u>Mr. Stone's</u> store early.
8. Mother, take <u>Mother's</u> car keys.
9. The scottie is <u>Rick and Mindy's</u> dog.
10. Leroy and Wayne invited Paul to <u>Leroy and Wayne's</u> magic show.

**D. Using Pronouns Correctly** Number your paper from 1 to 10. Write the correct word for each sentence.

1. Can we bake at (their, there) house?
2. (It's, Its) too cold to go swimming.
3. The snake shed (its, it's) skin.
4. Babe Ruth played baseball (their, there).
5. The tiger swung (it's, its) paw.
6. (They're, Their) flowers need water.
7. (Its, It's) finally stopped snowing.
8. (There, They're) looking for butterflies.
9. My canary tries to leave (it's, its) cage.
10. Ms. Yu made up (they're, their) faces for the play.

# Using Grammar in Writing

**A.** Something strange happened yesterday. At school there was somebody who looked just like you. The person was wearing clothes like yours. Everywhere you went, that person went too. The person even said what you said. Write a paragraph telling about your strange day.

**B.** A giraffe wandered from the zoo. The giraffe got hungry. It found some plants to eat on the second floor of a building. The people had left the windows open. That building is your house. Tell about seeing a giraffe in your window.

**C. Using Pronouns in Social Studies** A city has many community helpers. Some of them are police officers. Police officers do many things to help people. They direct traffic. They help children who are lost. Write about some other things police officers do to help us.

# Chapter 7 Review

**A. Choosing the Correct Pronoun** Number your paper from 1 to 10. Write the correct pronoun for each sentence.

1. Will you hold the paintbrush for (I, me)?
2. Fred and (her, she) washed the car.
3. (Us, We) can't help you fix the guitar.
4. Carrie pushed the wheelchair for (he, him).
5. (Them, They) can swim for ten minutes.
6. Do you have an extra dime for (him, his)?
7. Mom made a costume for (she, her).
8. Julio steered the sailboat toward (us, we).
9. (They, Them) planted a garden together.
10. Grandfather and (me, I) hiked two miles.

**B. Using Pronouns Correctly** Each sentence below has a mistake in it. Write the sentences correctly.

1. There talent show lasted an hour.
2. Jim and me watched the blastoff.
3. Dad made pancakes for Tanya and I.
4. The collie brings Shari it's leash.
5. Our science club meets they're.

**C. Writing with Pronouns** Write this paragraph, using pronouns for the underlined words.

Giant pandas come from China. Some zoos have <u>pandas</u>. A panda is a large black and white animal. <u>A panda</u> has small black ears. <u>Pandas'</u> eyes have black patches around them. People say <u>pandas</u> are like bears.

# Chapter 8

# Telling a Story

Suppose you are telling a story. You reach this part.

> "Suddenly all the lights went out! All I could see was a shadow moving toward me."

How would you say these sentences? Would you use your face or hands? Good storytellers help the audience feel what is happening. They help their listeners picture the events in the story.

In this chapter, you will learn the parts of a story. You will tell a story about yourself and make up a class story. You will learn about fables and tall tales. You will find out how to make your stories exciting.

# 1 Discovering the Parts of a Story

> A story has three parts. They are the **beginning,** the **middle,** and the **end.**

A good story keeps the listener's attention from beginning to end. Whether a story is long or short, it should have three main parts.

The **beginning** sentences get the story started. The first sentences answer many of the **W** questions: *Who? What? Where? When? Why?*

The **middle** of the story contains the action. Each sentence in the middle tells about something that happens. The action builds up to the **climax,** the most exciting part of the story.

The **end** of the story tells how everything works out. The last sentences tie the whole story together.

Look at the following fable. A **fable** is a make-believe story that teaches a lesson. The lesson is called a **moral.** This fable was written by a man named Aesop more than two thousand years ago.

See if Aesop's fable has a beginning, a middle, and an end. Try to figure out the lesson it teaches.

### The Shepherd Boy and the Wolf

A shepherd boy was tending his flock of sheep near a village. He decided to play a joke on the villagers by pretending a wolf was attacking the sheep. He shouted, "Wolf! Wolf!"

When the people came to help, he laughed at them. He played the trick again and again.

One day a wolf really did come. The boy cried, "Wolf! Wolf!" as loud as he could. But the people paid no attention. Nobody believed him when he really needed help. The wolf dragged off one of the sheep.

Never again did the boy play tricks on the villagers. He had learned his lesson, and a sad one it was.

## Exercises  Discovering the Parts of a Story

**A.** Look at the beginning of Aesop's story. Answer these **W** questions.

1. **Who** was the story about?
2. **What** was the person doing?
3. **Where** does the story take place?

**B.** Look at the middle and the end of the story. Answer these questions.

1. What is the climax of the story?
2. What sentence or sentences tie the whole story together?

**C.** Here is a sentence that tells the moral of the story. Write the sentence. Use these words to fill in the blanks.

believe    truth    lies

"When people tell _____ often, it is hard to _____ them when they tell the _____."

# 2 Reading a Story Aloud

> When you read a story aloud, speak clearly.
> Show feelings so the characters will seem real.

The person who tells a story can make it come alive. Whether you read a story from a book or tell one that you have made up, help your listeners enjoy it. Here are some things to do.

**1. Learn new words.** Before you share a story with others, make sure you know all the words. Look up words you don't know. Practice saying words that are hard. Here are a few words from "The Shepherd Boy and the Wolf." Do you know their meanings?

    tend    shepherd    flock    village

**2. Take your time and speak clearly.** Don't rush when you read aloud. Give your listeners plenty of time. They need to hear every word. They also need time to think about what is happening in the story. Speak clearly so that people will understand what you say.

**3. Show feelings to make the characters seem real.** When you speak, make the words come alive. Use your voice, your face, and your hands to express feelings.

In the story "The Shepherd Boy and the Wolf," there are at least two places where the storyteller can show feelings.

He shouted, "Wolf, Wolf!"

The boy cried, "Wolf! Wolf!" as loud as he could.

You don't actually have to shout the words, but you can say them with strong feelings.

**Guides for Telling a Story**

1. Learn the new words.
2. Take your time and speak clearly.
3. Show feelings to make characters seem real.

## Exercises   Reading a Story Aloud

**A.** Read these sentences silently. Think about them. Then take turns reading the sentences aloud. Show feelings.

1. Slowly, the snake wriggled through the grass. It came closer and closer. I couldn't move.
2. "Ha!" she laughed. "You aren't a real monster. You were just trying to fool me!"
3. "Really, Mr. Brown, you must be wrong. My dog is big, but he never bites."

**B.** Form groups of three. Take turns reading "The Shepherd Boy and the Wolf". Follow the Guides for Telling a Story. Ask the others in your group to tell you how well you read.

**C.** Find a book of fables in your school library. Choose a fable to tell to a group. In some books, the moral is at the end of the fable. Do not tell the moral right away; see if your listeners can figure it out.

## 3  Telling a Story About Yourself

> When you tell a story about yourself, plan the story. List the events in order.

Can you think of a story to tell about yourself? Try to remember something that happened to you. The event can be funny or serious.

### Planning Your Story

After you decide on an idea, plan the beginning of your story. Include some answers to the **W** questions.

Now plan the middle of the story. Think about the action and the climax. Then think of an ending to tie the story together.

### Listing Events in Order

Your listeners will enjoy your story if it is easy to follow. Make a list of the events in order. Read this list that Marsha wrote. Then read her story.

1. Last summer we drove to the mountains.
2. We stopped for lunch.
3. Mom thought my brother and sister were lost.
4. They were playing behind some rocks.

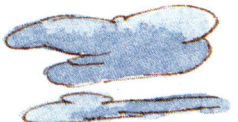

### A Mountain Scare

Last summer Mom, Dad, Hank, Patty, and I took a trip. We visited the Rocky Mountains.

One day we were driving in the mountains. We stopped to have our picnic lunch. My little brother and sister walked over to a rock to play. When Mom looked up, she couldn't see Hank and Patty anywhere! Mom was scared. She screamed and ran toward the rock.

Just then, Patty and Hank stuck their heads up over the rock. They had been safe all along. Mom was upset, though. She and Dad kept us close to them during the rest of the trip.

**Exercises**  **Telling a Story About Yourself**

**A.** Think about Marsha's story. Answer these questions.

1. Tell the answers to the **W** questions at the beginning: *Who? What? When?*
2. How did Mom feel when she couldn't see Hank and Patty?
3. What did Marsha's parents do during the rest of the trip?

**B.** Plan a story about yourself. List the events in order. Answer as many **W** questions as you can. Lead your story into a climax. Then think of a good ending.

Tell your story to a group. Speak clearly. Use your voice and hands to show feelings.

Listen to your classmates' stories. Pay careful attention so you will hear everything.

# 4 Telling a Class Story

> A **class story** is one in which everyone shares ideas.

You and your class can tell a story together. Each person can tell an idea. A good story for the class to work on can be a tall tale. A **tall tale** is a funny story about someone who can do impossible things.

In the early days of America, the settlers made up stories about heroes who did wild, unbelievable things. You may have heard about one of the heroes, Paul Bunyan. Here is part of a Paul Bunyan story.

Paul Bunyan was a giant lumberjack. He was so big, he could put trees into his pockets. One day he wanted to make pancakes for the other lumberjacks. He needed a griddle big enough for one hundred pancakes. Paul built a griddle so huge there was no wagon to carry it. He had to roll it from Maine to Minnesota.

To begin a class story, talk together about the **W** questions. Create your main character. Name the events that will fill the middle of the tall tale. Then decide together how to end the story.

Follow the Guides for Writing and Telling a Class Story that appear on the next page.

> **Guides for Writing and Telling a Class Story**
>
> 1. Talk together about the beginning, middle, and end.
> 2. Let everyone make up a sentence to go into the story.
> 3. Arrange the sentences in an order that makes sense.
> 4. Combine ideas. Take out sentences that don't fit.
> 5. Reread the whole story together.

## Exercises   Telling a Class Story

**A.** Work with your classmates to plan a tall tale. First, decide on the answers to these questions.

1. **Who** will be the main character?
2. **What** impossible things will he or she do?
3. **Where** does the story take place?
4. **When** does the story take place?
5. **Why** is the main character special?

Next, tell about the middle of the tall tale. Begin by answering these questions together.

1. What adventure does the main character have?
2. What is the most unbelievable thing that happens?

Finally, talk together about the end of the tall tale. How will you bring everything together?

**B.** Your class is ready to tell a class story. Take turns telling the tall tale. Your class may want to draw pictures to go with the tall tale. Some class members might like to act it out for the rest of the class.

# Using English in Drama

There are many ways to tell a story. A story may be written or spoken aloud. A story may also be told as a drama or a play.

## Exercise  Presenting a Play

Work with a group of friends to give a play. Choose a story that you would like to act out. It may be a story from your reading book, a fairy tale, or a tall tale. Then look at these four important parts of a play. Follow the suggestions.

**Story** Work together to plan the play from the story. Decide what the characters will say. You may want to write what everyone says.

**Actors** Decide who will play each character.

**Costumes** If you need costumes, you can make them from paper or old clothes.

**Setting** The setting is the place where the play happens. Make a big picture of the setting. Hang it on the wall behind the actors. You may need some furniture, dishes, or other things the characters use.

Practice your play. The actors should think about how their characters would look, talk, move, and feel. Each actor should learn the part he or she is playing. Speak clearly so that everyone can hear.

When your play is ready, perform it for the class.

# Chapter 8 Review

**A. Finding the Parts of a Story** Read this fable. Write the answers to the questions that follow it.

### Belling the Cat

Five mice and one cat lived in a big old house. The mice were always bothered by the cat. They got together to decide what to do. One mouse said, "If the cat had a bell on her collar, we could hear her coming. Then we could run away."

All the mice thought this was a fine idea. But there was a problem. Who would put the bell on the cat?

1. Who are the characters in the story?
2. Where does the story take place?
3. What is the lesson, or moral, in the fable?

**B. Telling a Story** Write these five sentences about storytelling. Use the words to complete the sentences.

    ideas    new    everyone
    speak    time    feelings

1. Before you tell a story, learn the _____ words.
2. Take your _____ and _____ clearly.
3. Help the listeners by showing _____ with your voice.
4. Let _____ write part of a class story.
5. Your class should combine _____.

# Chapter 9

# Learning About Verbs

Imagine that you are doing exercises. These sentences tell some of the things you might do.

You stretch.   You twist.
You bend.     You jump.

Now imagine that you are standing still.

You see.      You think.
You hear.     You breathe.

In each of these sentences, the pronoun *you* names a person. The other word is a verb. The verb tells what you are doing. Even when you are standing still, you are doing something.

In this chapter, you will learn about many ways that verbs are used. You will see how verbs tell what is happening now and what has already happened.

# 1 What Are Verbs?

> A **verb** tells what a person or thing does.

Words that tell about action are called **verbs**. Look at these sentences.

Carl <u>climbs</u> trees.    Lynn <u>jumps</u> rope.

The underlined words tell what each person is doing. Those words are verbs. Some verbs tell about an action you can see. *Climbs* and *jumps* are this kind of verb.

Some verbs tell about action you cannot see.

Nancy <u>wishes</u> for snow.    Kenji <u>likes</u> music.

You can't see people *wish* or *like*. Can you think of some other things people do that you cannot see?

In Chapter 4, you learned that a sentence has a subject and a predicate. The predicate tells what the subject does. Every predicate must have a verb in it.

| Subject | Predicate |
|---|---|
| Peggy | <u>sneezes</u>. |
| Jim | <u>wants</u> cheese. |
| The kite | <u>landed</u> in the tree. |

Some predicates have more than one word. Other predicates have only one word. That one word must be a verb. Every sentence must have a verb.

## Exercises   Finding Verbs

**A.** Find the verbs in these sentences. Write the verbs.

1. The kitten purrs.
2. My friend and I pulled weeds.
3. Stars twinkle in the sky.
4. The painter climbed the ladder.
5. Kristen threw the ball.
6. The sailboat floated away.
7. I saw the new train station.
8. Arthur spent all of his money.
9. My cousin caught a big fish.
10. Louise dropped the package.

**B.** Here are ten groups of words. Each group needs a verb in order to be a sentence. Think of a verb for each group of words. Write your sentence.

1. Jerry _____ his toes.
2. Mice _____ cheese.
3. Fran _____ an apple.
4. The bird _____ a nest.
5. Dentists _____ teeth.
6. Firefighters _____ hoses.
7. Rita _____ the present.
8. Dogs _____ their tails.
9. Pilots _____ planes.
10. Did you _____ Douglas?

**C. Writing** Imagine you are watching an exciting baseball game. Write about the people watching the game. How do they act? How do they feel about their team?

# 2 Two Kinds of Verbs

> Some verbs tell what a person or thing **does**.
> Other verbs say that something **is**.

Not all verbs do the same job. There are two different kinds of verbs. They do two different jobs.

## Action Verbs

You learned about action verbs in part 1. **Action verbs** tell what a person or thing *does*.

Kim <u>waved</u>.    Her balloons <u>sailed</u> away.

Some action verbs tell about actions you can see. Others tell about actions you cannot see.

Grandma <u>hoped</u> for rain.

## Verbs That Say That Something Is

Not all verbs are action verbs. For example, read the following sentences.

The sun <u>is</u> hot.    The crows <u>are</u> noisy.

The first sentence tells about the sun. However, it does not say that the sun does anything. It simply says what the sun *is*. The second sentence tells about crows. It says what the crows *are*.

*Is* and *are* are **verbs that tell that something is**. They are examples of the second kind of verb.

## Forms of the Verb *Be*

The verbs that say that something **is** are all forms of the verb *be*. The verb *be* is used more than any other verb. If you use its forms correctly, other people will understand you better.

Here are some of the forms of the verb *be*.

**am    is    are    was    were**

Sometimes you may not know which form of *be* to use. Think about the subject of your sentence. The right form of the verb depends on the subject. Study the following chart. It shows how to use these forms of *be* correctly.

| Subject | Verb | Sample Sentence |
|---|---|---|
| **I** | **am** <br> or <br> **was** | I am early today. <br> <br> I was late yesterday. |
| **you** | **are** <br> or <br> **were** | You are tall now. <br> <br> You were short last year. |
| any other singular noun or pronoun | **is** <br> or <br> **was** | Gloria is my neighbor. <br> <br> She was at my party. |
| any other plural noun or pronoun | **are** <br> or <br> **were** | The streets are dry now. <br> <br> They were wet last night. |

**Exercises**  **Using Two Kinds of Verbs**

**A.** Write the verbs from the following sentences. Then write **A** for action verbs or **I** for verbs that say something is.

1. The baby chicks are so soft.
2. Cherie started the video game.
3. An elf owl is very small.
4. I took an airplane ride.
5. The officer used his flashlight.
6. Gilberto laughed at the clown.
7. The *Mayflower* is the name of a ship.
8. The parrot cage was empty.
9. My costume sparkled.
10. The bear cubs were sleepy.

**B.** Choose the correct form of **be** for these sentences. Write the sentences.

1. I (was, be) afraid of the dark.
2. You (is, are) too old for this toy.
3. Karen (am, is) proud of her work.
4. You (was, were) first in line.
5. The crickets (is, are) noisy.

**C. Writing** Crickets make a loud chirping noise. Other insects and animals also make special noises. Can you think of some? Write about some animal sounds you have heard. Use action verbs and forms of the verb *be*.

# 3 Main Verbs and Helping Verbs

> Sometimes a verb has more than one word.
> The most important word is called the **main verb.**
> The other words in the verb are called **helping verbs.**

In many sentences, there is only one word in the verb.

Ron *talked* with Linda.

In other sentences, there are two, or three, or even four words in the verb.

Ron *was talking* with Linda.
Ron *should have talked* with Linda.
Ron *must have been talking* with Linda.

This chart shows the main verbs and the helping verbs in the sample sentences.

| Helping Verbs | Main Verbs |
|---:|:---|
| was | talking |
| should have | talked |
| must have been | talking |

There are several helping verbs. However, some groups of helping verbs are used more often than others. Study this chart.

| Verbs often used as helping verbs | | | | |
|---|---|---|---|---|
| am | was | has | do | can |
| is | were | have | does | could |
| are | will | had | did | may |

## Verbs That Need Helping Verbs

Some verbs need helping verbs. It is incorrect to use these verbs by themselves. Verbs that end in *-en* or *-ing* usually need helping verbs.

| eaten | I *have eaten* all the fruit. |
| driven | My father *has driven* to Detroit. |
| singing | The students *were singing*. |
| drinking | Jan *is drinking* her milk. |

Later in this chapter, you will learn more about **verbs that need helping verbs.**

## Exercises  Finding Main Verbs and Helping Verbs

**A.** Write these two headings: **Helping Verbs, Main Verbs.** Find the verbs in these sentences. Write the helping verbs and the main verbs under the correct headings.

1. Yolanda will feed the goldfish.
2. The plane was circling the airport.
3. Freddy has been whistling that tune.
4. Dad and Kathy were making a doghouse.
5. The squirrels have been hiding the nuts.
6. My sister was playing a math game.
7. Sheila is practicing the piano.
8. Kevin may have fallen in the mud.
9. Texas is called the Lone Star State.
10. He should have worn a jacket.

**B.** Think of a verb for each blank. Write the sentences.

1. The puppies were _____ in circles.
2. Milito will _____ after lunch.
3. Your cat was _____ under the porch.
4. Zachary may be _____ a poster.
5. A frog was _____ on that log.
6. Pauline has _____ to the library.
7. Mr. Carlson is _____ the floor.
8. Our club members are _____ seeds.
9. Ella may be _____ to Portland.
10. The parrots have _____ all the food.

**C. Writing** Do you like to tell jokes? Think of a funny joke. Write it for a friend. Use helping verbs in your sentences.

# 4 Verbs That Tell About Present Time

> Verbs that tell about things happening right now are in the **present time.**

Some verbs tell about things that are happening right now. Here are some examples.

Ted *is* at a concert. He *listens* to a band.
Jill *has* a hobby. She *collects* model cars.

We say that verbs like these are in the **present time.** Verbs in the present time have two forms. One form is the basic form. Examples are *ride*, *play*, and *see*.

The other form is the basic form with an *s* added, called the **-s** form. Examples are *rides*, *plays*, and *sees*. There is only one correct verb form for each sentence. The form depends on the subject of the sentence.

Keith *rides* his bike.
The boys *ride* their bikes.

Libby *plays* baseball.
The girls *play* baseball.

The rabbit *sees* the garden.
The rabbits *see* the garden.

> Use the **-s** form of a verb with a singular subject.
> Use the basic form of a verb with a plural subject.

## Verbs With *I* and *You*

Verbs used with the pronouns *I* and *you* do not follow the rule at the bottom of page 136. The word *I* stands for one person. The word *you* may stand for one or more than one person. However, *I* and *you* are always used with the basic form of a verb.

I *ride* my bike.    You *ride* your bike.

## Spelling Changes

Sometimes, you must make spelling changes to verbs when you write the *-s* form. Follow these rules.

**1. If the basic verb form ends in *s, x, ch,* or *sh,* add *-es* to make the *-s* form.**

- **s**  The players *pass* the ball.
  Juan *passes* the ball.

- **x**  The workers *fix* radios.
  Carla *fixes* radios.

- **ch**  The butterflies *touch* the flowers.
  The butterfly *touches* the flowers.

- **sh**  The shoppers *push* the carts.
  Each shopper *pushes* a cart.

**2. Some verbs have a basic form that ends in *y* following a consonant. Change the *y* to *i* and add *-es*.**

The horses *carry* riders.
My horse *carries* me.

## Exercises  Using Verbs That Tell About Present Time

**A.** Write the subject and the verb from the following sentences. Tell whether the subject is **singular** or **plural.**

Example: The players need a rest.
players need—plural

1. Leaves change color in the fall.
2. The people hear the bells on Sunday.
3. Farah carries the heavy basket easily.
4. Your book tells facts about insects.
5. This key opens the treasure chest.
6. My sisters practice every day.
7. That door closes too quickly.
8. Airplanes fly over my house.
9. We enjoy band concerts.
10. Glen reads about famous Americans.

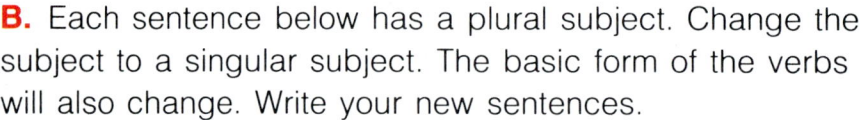

**B.** Each sentence below has a plural subject. Change the subject to a singular subject. The basic form of the verbs will also change. Write your new sentences.

Example: The giraffes watch the visitors.
The giraffe watches the visitors.

1. The cooks mix the vegetables.
2. My kittens worry my mother.
3. Grandpa's neighbors wash his car.
4. The scouts toss the boomerang.
5. Her photos show many animals.

**C. Writing** Tell about jobs you can do to help younger or older people. Use verbs in the present time.

# 5 Verbs That Tell About Past Time

> Verbs that tell about something that has already happened are in the **past time**.

Some verbs tell about something that has already happened. Here are some examples.

Ted *helped* his mother. He *cooked* dinner.

We say that verbs like this are in the **past time**. There are three ways you can show past time.

**1. Adding -ed to the Basic Form** You can make most verbs tell about the past by adding *-ed* to the basic form.

    cook    cooked    laugh    laughed

Often you must make spelling changes. Follow these rules when you write verbs in the past time.

- When the basic form ends in silent *e*, drop the final *e*. Then add *-ed*.

    rak<u>e</u>    rak<u>ed</u>    mov<u>e</u>    mov<u>ed</u>

- When the basic form ends in *y* after a consonant, change the *y* to *i*. Then add *-ed*.

    hurr<u>y</u>    hurr<u>ied</u>    cop<u>y</u>    cop<u>ied</u>

- When the basic form ends in a single consonant after a short vowel, double the final consonant. Then add *-ed*.

    sto<u>p</u>    sto<u>pped</u>    pa<u>t</u>    pa<u>tted</u>

**2. Using Helping Verbs** Another way to make verbs show the past is to use helping verbs. You use **has** or **have** or **had** with the *-ed* form of the verb.

Vincent *studied* the violin.
He *has studied* for a year.

Faith and Eddie *worked* on a report.
They *have worked* together before.

Donna *laughed* at the clown.
She *had laughed* at all his tricks.

Use **has** with a singular subject. Use **have** with a plural subject and the pronoun *I*. Use **had** with either a singular or a plural subject.

**3. Changing the Basic Form** Some verbs change their basic form to show past time. Some of those verbs change their form again to show past time with a helping verb.

| Present | Past | Past with Helping Verb |
|---------|------|------------------------|
| come    | came | have come              |
| see     | saw  | have seen              |
| is      | was  | has been               |
| are     | were | have been              |

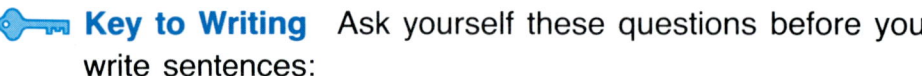 **Key to Writing** Ask yourself these questions before you write sentences:
  Am I telling about something happening now? (present)
  Am I telling about something that already happened? (past)
Your answer will help you choose the correct verbs.

# Exercises  Using Verbs That Tell About Past Time

**A.** Write these verbs. Show past time by adding **-ed**. Make any spelling change that is needed.

Example: tap   tapped

1. walk
2. play
3. hop
4. cry
5. smile
6. taste
7. use
8. show
9. rip
10. invite
11. push
12. try
13. train
14. carry
15. pin

**B.** Each sentence below should tell about something that happened in the past. Choose the correct verb. Write the sentences.

1. Birdseed (was, is) all over the cage.
2. Amy and Jorge (come, came) to karate class.
3. I (have been, are) tired ever since our trip.
4. They (sip, had sipped) their drinks slowly.
5. Your class (seen, has seen) that movie.
6. On her last birthday Leah (is, was) eight.
7. Miss Chu (had read, reads) my poem two days ago.
8. Uncle Fred (visit, visited) us last Sunday.
9. Dan (saw, see) the frog before it jumped.
10. The vines (climb, have climbed) up the garden wall.

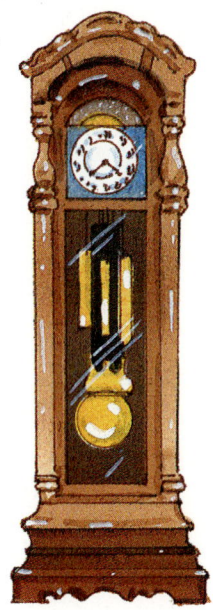

**C. Writing** Think of a special day in the past. Perhaps there was a day when you learned to do something special. Write about what happened that day.

# 6  More Verbs That Change Their Form

> Many verbs change their form to tell about the past. It is important to learn the forms of those verbs.

You have learned that the verbs *am, is, are, come,* and *see* change their form to show past time. Our language has many other verbs that change form.

Look at the following sentences. They use different forms of the verb *eat.*

> The puppy **eats** quickly. (present)
> The puppy **ate** quickly. (past alone)
> The puppy **has eaten.** (past with helping verb)

The verb *eats* tells what the puppy is doing now. The verb *ate* tells what the puppy did in the past. The verb *eaten* is used with a helping verb to tell what the puppy did in the past.

Here is a chart that shows how other verbs change their form. It is important to learn these verbs so that you can use them correctly.

| Present | Past Alone | Past with Helping Verb |
|---------|------------|------------------------|
| do      | did        | (have) done            |
| go      | went       | (have) gone            |
| run     | ran        | (have) run             |
| give    | gave       | (have) given           |
| take    | took       | (have) taken           |
| break   | broke      | (have) broken          |

## Exercises  Using Verbs That Change Their Form

**A.** Choose the correct verb in each sentence. Write the verbs.

1. I have (saw, seen) that movie three times.
2. Carol (gone, went) to the record shop.
3. Gary has (do, done) his homework.
4. The birds have (ate, eaten) the cherries.
5. Have you (been, was) to the county fair?
6. My cat has (took, taken) all the yarn out.
7. Fred's radio (broken, broke) when it dropped.
8. We (ran, run) back for our sled.
9. Mom (was, been) in a good mood.
10. Ms. Porter (gave, give) you a part in the play.

**B.** These sentences use verbs in the present time. Write each sentence, changing the verb to show past time. Use the past form without the helping verb.

1. Our hamsters eat vegetables.
2. Uncle Bob sees a robin in the yard.
3. I take a new path to school.
4. Juanita gives apples to Katrina.
5. Ted goes to a boat race on Tuesday.

# 7 Using Contractions

> A **contraction** is a shortened form of two words. An apostrophe takes the place of missing letters.

We often use a shortened form of two words, called a **contraction**. When the words are put together, at least one letter is left out. An apostrophe (') is used in place of the missing letters.

<u>I</u> <u>wi</u>ll   becomes   <u>I</u>'<u>ll</u>
<u>she</u> <u>is</u>   becomes   <u>she</u>'<u>s</u>
<u>they</u> <u>are</u>   becomes   <u>they</u>'<u>re</u>
<u>we</u> <u>have</u>   becomes   <u>we</u>'<u>ve</u>

Notice how the underlined letters are used to form the contraction. The letters that are not underlined are not used in the contraction. An apostrophe is used instead.

Many contractions are made by putting together a pronoun and a verb. Read this list of contractions. Notice where the apostrophes are used.

| I am | I'm | we are | we're |
| I have | I've | we had | we'd |
| I will | I'll | we will | we'll |
| you are | you're | you will | you'll |
| he is | he's | you have | you've |
| she will | she'll | they had | they'd |
| it is | it's | they will | they'll |

**It's** real.    It **isn't**.

Other contractions are made by putting together a verb and the word *not*. In the following contractions, *not* always becomes *n't*.

| is not | isn't | has not | hasn't |
| are not | aren't | have not | haven't |
| was not | wasn't | had not | hadn't |
| were not | weren't | can not | can't |
| could not | couldn't | do not | don't |
| would not | wouldn't | does not | doesn't |
| should not | shouldn't | did not | didn't |

The words *will* and *not* form the contraction *won't*. This is the only contraction used often in which letters are dropped and other letters are changed.

*won't*

## Exercises   Using Contractions

**A.** Copy the following contractions. After each, write the two words that formed the contraction.

1. you've
2. aren't
3. wasn't
4. I've
5. they'll
6. shouldn't
7. haven't
8. won't
9. we're
10. we'll

**B.** In each sentence below, two words are underlined. Write the sentences, changing the two words into a contraction.

1. Jeff <u>can not</u> find his ski mask.
2. <u>You will</u> enjoy the band concert.
3. <u>Do not</u> forget my slumber party.
4. <u>I am</u> planning to do my science project.
5. Do you think <u>they are</u> coming soon?
6. If <u>you are</u> old enough, you can join.
7. Tamara <u>could not</u> reach the shelf.
8. <u>He is</u> telling jokes for the program.
9. Dad said <u>it is</u> too early to go fishing.
10. The sun <u>is not</u> shining today.

**C. Writing** Imagine there are traffic lights on all the doors in your house. Write a set of rules to go with the lights. Use contractions in your rules.

# 8 Using Negatives Correctly

> The *not-words* and *no-words* are called **negatives.**
> Do not use two negatives in the same sentence.

You have learned that some contractions are made by putting together a verb and the word *not*. Words made in this way are called **not-words.**

was + not = wasn't    did + not = didn't

There are some other words called **no-words.** Each of these words, except one, has *no* in it.

| no | nobody | none | never |
|---|---|---|---|
| no one | nothing | nowhere | |

*Not-words* and *no-words* are called **negatives.** Do not use two negatives together in a sentence.

Wrong: **Don't be no litterbug!**
Right: **Don't be a litterbug!**

## Exercise  Using Negatives Correctly

Write each of these sentences. Use the correct word.

1. There aren't (no, any) letters for me.
2. I don't (ever, never) get sick.
3. Most spiders don't hurt (anybody, nobody).
4. Roberto doesn't remember (nothing, anything).
5. I (haven't, have) never ridden an elephant.

# Exercises for Mastery   Chapter 9

**A. Finding Verbs** Copy the following sentences. Underline the verb in each sentence.

1. Hens lay eggs every day.
2. The wind blew hard.
3. The tiger roared loudly.
4. Mom sells new houses.
5. Van loved the black puppy.
6. The rabbit hopped away.
7. Travis does magic tricks.
8. My favorite show begins now.
9. Our class gave a Halloween play.
10. Birds fly south in the fall.

**B. Using Two Kinds of Verbs** Write the verbs in these sentences. Then tell what kind of verb each one is. Write **A** for action verbs or **I** for verbs that say something *is*.

Examples: Hannah played the piano.  played  **A**
Uncle Brad was a sailor.  was  **I**

1. The planets move around the sun.
2. I am sure about that answer.
3. The directions were clear.
4. An engineer drives the train.
5. The cashier gave me my ticket.
6. Danny is twelve years old.
7. You are very friendly.
8. The hawk flew high.
9. My vacation was too short.
10. Shelly wore her new boots.

**C. Using Helping Verbs** Write the following sentences. Draw one line under the helping verb and two lines under the main verb.

1. Bill has been a Cub Scout for one year.
2. Carter and Janet have gone to a science fair.
3. Some drivers are honking their horns.
4. The arrow is pointing north.
5. Marla and Lucy are jumping rope.
6. Spencer was writing a letter.
7. The wind has blown the paper away.
8. A mountain climber has broken his leg.
9. Tanya had crawled under the table.
10. Misako is bouncing the ball.

**D. Using Verbs That Tell About Present Time** Choose the correct form of the verb in each sentence. Write the verb.

1. Steve (likes, like) bananas.
2. These shoes (costs, cost) too much.
3. Kimberly (collect, collects) coins.
4. Mr. Maxwell (fix, fixes) clocks.
5. Children (love, loves) parades.
6. Dogs (barks, bark) at strangers.
7. Mary (dislike, dislikes) red shoes.
8. Ants always (comes, come) to our picnics.
9. Shadows (grow, grows) long in the afternoon.
10. The elevator (stops, stop) on the first floor.

# Exercises for Mastery  Continued

**E. Using Verbs That Tell About Past Time** Choose the form of the verb that shows past time correctly. Write the verb.

1. The lion (washed, washing) its paws.
2. Sammy (done, has done) his best.
3. Kareem and Lorna (hurryed, hurried) to Grandfather's store.
4. Mrs. Potter (had read, reads) my story two weeks ago.
5. We (studyed, studied) about the pilgrims.
6. Casey has been (raking, rake) the leaves.
7. Our postal worker (carry, carried) a heavy sack.
8. The car suddenly (stopped, stoped).
9. Maria (stays, stayed) home yesterday.
10. The farmer (plants, planted) corn last spring.

**F. Using Verbs That Change Their Form** Choose the correct verb for each sentence. Write the sentences.

1. Joseph (gone, went) to swimming class.
2. The window was (broke, broken) before we moved in.
3. Have you ever (saw, seen) any kangaroos?
4. I (eaten, ate) dinner at Danielle's house.
5. Aunt Bea (gives, gave) me a book last week.
6. Mr. Long has (went, gone) to Alaska for the summer.

7. What (taken, took) you so long?
8. Many parents have (came, come) to the Open House.
9. Who (was, were) those people you visited?
10. My pet gerbil (ran, run) out of its cage last night.

**G. Using Contractions** Read each of the following pairs of words. Write each pair of words as a contraction.

1. do not
2. had not
3. she is
4. were not
5. can not
6. is not
7. he has
8. they are
9. I have
10. could not

**H. Using Negatives** Write each sentence below. Choose the correct word.

1. Maria's spelling test hasn't (no, any) errors.
2. Can't (nobody, anybody) fix this fence?
3. I don't (ever, never) come early.
4. Anna won't smile at (anybody, nobody).
5. Jeremy has (ever, never) been to my house.
6. Our team hasn't scored (any, no) points.
7. The bare tree doesn't give (no, any) shade.
8. My brother won't (never, ever) eat onions.
9. I don't need (no, any) help.
10. The desk didn't have (anything, nothing) in it.

# Using Grammar in Writing

**A.** Fiona has a fantastic garden. She grows roses, petunias, and daisies. Her flowers do fantastic things. Fiona's **r**oses **r**ide **r**oller coasters! Her **p**etunias **p**eel **p**otatoes! Her **d**aisies **d**ig **d**irt. Continue the story of Fiona's fantastic garden. Use tulips, lilies, and begonias. Follow the pattern. Tell what fantastic things her other flowers do.

**B.** Larry writes about his new puppy. He writes a story in the present time. Larry tells what his puppy is doing now.

> I have a new puppy. He cries all night. Mom understands. She says he misses his family. We think she is right.

It is one month later. Write Larry's story about his puppy. Change all of the verbs to show past time.

**C. Using Verbs in Health** Dr. Smiley, your dentist, has asked you to write what to do when you brush your teeth. Make a step-by-step list. Begin each sentence with an action verb.

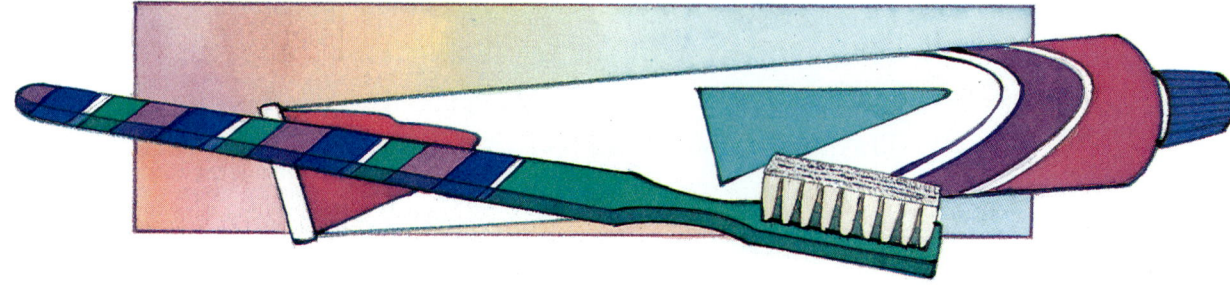

# Chapter 9 Review

**A. Finding Verbs in the Present Time and Past Time**
Write the verbs from the following sentences. Include any helping verbs. Write **Present** or **Past** after each verb.

1. Hobbies are fun to share.
2. Grandfather took us to the museum.
3. Your glove is on the floor.
4. Many branches were broken in the storm.
5. Tasha tells Luis about dolphins.
6. Mr. Lopez opened the school on Sunday.
7. That neighbor borrowed our tools.
8. Joanna jumps higher than Bruce.
9. We ate all of the popcorn.
10. Uncle Pete is cleaning the fish tank.

**B. Using Contractions and Negatives** Rewrite these sentences. Choose the correct word. Change each of the underlined pairs to a contraction.

Example: You <u>have not</u> lost (nothing, anything).
You haven't lost anything.

1. <u>Do not</u> tell (no one, anyone) this secret.
2. I <u>did not</u> forget (nothing, anything).
3. David <u>can not</u> go (anywhere, nowhere).
4. My cat <u>will not</u> (ever, never) sleep outdoors.
5. The store <u>does not</u> sell (any, no) light bulbs.
6. I <u>do not</u> want (any, none) of that fruit.
7. Jean <u>has not</u> (ever, never) been tardy.
8. I <u>have</u> never won (nothing, anything).
9. My sister <u>will not</u> sing (any, no) songs.
10. You <u>should not</u> leave (any, no) lights on.

153

# Chapter 10

# Writing a Story

Do you like mystery stories? Have you ever read about creatures from other planets? Do you know any stories about the time before people had cars or telephones?

There are many different kinds of stories. They may be about things that really happened or about something make-believe. Yet all stories are alike in some ways. In every story something happens. It happens to someone. It happens somewhere.

Stories may be told in different ways. You can tell a story aloud. You can sing a story. You can also write a story. In this chapter, you will learn about writing stories. You will learn how to plan a story and make it interesting for others to read.

# 1 Thinking About Stories

> A story tells about something that happens. A story has characters and a setting.

A story tells about something that happens to someone. That someone is called a **character.** There is often more than one character in a story. The place where the story happens is called the **setting.**

Stories can be real or make-believe. Suppose your teacher asks you to write about something that really happened to you. What would you write about?

## Example 1

**Read and Think.** Rosa wrote a story about raking leaves. She uses the word *I* to tell about herself.

> Our yard had a million leaves. It took me two hours to rake the leaves into big piles. Then I began to jump and roll in the leaves. I was having fun. Suddenly the wind started to blow. All the piles disappeared. I had to rake a million leaves again.

**Think and Discuss.** Read these questions. Talk about the answers with your classmates.

1. Is the story real or make-believe?
2. What is the setting of the story?
3. Tell three things that happen in Rosa's story.

# Example 2

**Read and Think.** Rosa wrote a story about something real. Now read another story about something make-believe.

> Owl was at home. He was eating butter toast and hot pea soup for supper. Owl heard a loud sound at the front door. He opened his door wide. Winter came into the house. It came in fast. A cold wind pushed Owl against the wall. It blew out the fire in the fireplace. It made the window shades flap and shiver. It turned the pea soup into hard, green ice. The wind blew around and around. Then Winter rushed out and slammed the front door.
>
> —ARNOLD LOBEL

**Think and Discuss.** Here are some questions about this story. Answer the questions with your classmates.

1. Who are the characters in this story?
2. How can you tell that the owl story is make-believe?
3. Where does the story take place?
4. What happens in the story?

# 2  Parts of a Story

> A story has a beginning, a middle, and an end.

Every story has a beginning, a middle, and an end. Sometimes you need more than one paragraph to tell the parts of a story.

**Read and Think.** Read this story. The three paragraphs tell the beginning, middle, and end of the story. As you read, think about what each paragraph tells.

### Country Mouse Learns a Lesson

Country Mouse was poor. He had only stale bread and dry cheese to eat. His cousin City Mouse lived in a beautiful house. He nibbled the finest cheese. He ate raisin bread and apples every day.

City Mouse invited Country Mouse to visit his fine house. Country Mouse agreed. Late at night he arrived at his cousin's door. City Mouse led him to the kitchen. There they began to feast on leftovers from a big party. Suddenly, the mice heard barking. A huge dog rushed into the room. The mice barely escaped with their lives.

That same night Country Mouse went home. He had learned a lesson. He had learned that plain food, eaten in peace, tastes better than fine food, eaten without peace.

**Think and Discuss.** Talk about these questions with your class. Look back at the mouse story for help.

1. Who are the characters in the story?
2. What is the setting of the story?
3. Tell three things that happen in the story.
4. What part of the story does paragraph 3 tell?
5. Why does the story need three paragraphs?

## Exercise   Understanding a Story

Here is a story beginning. Talk with your classmates. Think of ideas for a middle and end to the story. Choose one of the ideas. Finish the story.

> I, Nate the Great, was drying off from the rain. I was sitting under a blanket and reading a detective book. My dog Sludge was sniffing it. I was on page 33 when I heard a knock. I opened the door.
>
> —MARJORIE WEINMAN SHARMAT

## Now It's Your Turn

You have read three stories that tell about something that happened. Each story had characters and a setting. One was about something real. Two were make-believe. You have seen that a story can be told in one or more paragraphs.

Now you will write your own story. You can write a real or a make-believe story. You will learn how to make your story fun for others to read.

# 3 Planning and Writing a Story

> Choose something to write about. Write notes about your idea. Then write a draft.

When you write a story, first think and plan. Use these prewriting steps to plan your story.

**1. Choose an idea for your story.** Here are some questions you can ask to think of an idea for your story.

- **Who will be the character?**
  A troll with big teeth?
  Your best friend?
  Yourself?

- **What will be the setting?**
  Your neighborhood?
  A make-believe land?
  A faraway place?

- **What will happen?**
  Something funny?
  Something scary?
  An exciting adventure?

Write all your ideas. Choose the characters, setting, and ideas you would like to write about.

160

**2. Write notes about your idea.** Write the main idea of the story you have chosen. Name the characters and setting. Then think about what happens. Plan your story so that it has a beginning, middle, and end.

Put your ideas in time order. Number the events in the order they happen.

**3. Write a draft.** Use your notes to write a draft. Your first sentences should name the characters and tell about the setting. Then, write the middle of your story. Tell everything that happens. Finally, write a sentence to end your story.

Use time words like *last year, before,* and *later* to show when the events happen.

Emily decided to write about the time her dog Fiddle fell in a mud hole. She put her prewriting notes in time order.

**Main idea**—the time Fiddle fell in a mud hole
**Characters**—me, Fiddle, cat
**Setting**—a muddy field

1. Fiddle chased a cat.
2. Fiddle disappeared.
3. I looked for him.
4. He fell in a mud hole.

Now Emily is ready to write a draft of her story.

## Exercise  Planning and Writing Your Draft

Choose an idea for your story. You may write about something real or make-believe. Brainstorm with your class to get ideas. Look at the **Power Handbook** for more ideas. Make notes. Plan your story. Then write your draft.

# 4 Revising and Sharing a Story

> Revise your story to make it better. Write a clean final copy to share.

Can you improve your draft? These guides will help you make your story better.

**Guides for Revising**

1. Does my story have a beginning, middle, and end?
2. Did I use the best words to tell what happened?
3. Have I told the events in the order they happened? Did I use time words to help?
4. Should I add anything to make the story clearer or more interesting?
5. Did I write good beginning and ending sentences?

Emily made these changes in her story. Do you see why she made each change?

(Make the beginning interesting.)

My dog Fiddle hates cats.
~~I have a dog named Fiddle.~~ One day he chased a cat across a muddy field. Suddenly, Fiddle disappeared. I ran to look for him. I found a big muddy hole. ~~Something~~ Some mud moved. It was Fiddle! Then ~~something~~ the mud barked. I pulled him out. We both looked like big mud monsters.

(I left out that it was Fiddle.)

(I need an ending.)

## Finishing Your Story

Proofread your draft for mistakes in capital letters, punctuation, and spelling. Make a clean copy in your best handwriting.

Write the title at the top of your paper. The title tells what the story is about. The first word of the title begins with a capital letter. All of the other important words do, too.

Here is Emily's final copy.

### The Mud Hole

My dog Fiddle hates cats. One day he chased a cat across a muddy field. Suddenly, Fiddle disappeared. I ran to look for him. I found a big muddy hole. Some mud moved. Then the mud barked. It was Fiddle! I pulled him out. We both looked like big mud monsters.

**Exercises** **Revising and Sharing Your Story**

**A. Finishing Your Story** Revise your draft to make it better. Use the Marks for Revising and Proofreading on page 331 of the **Power Handbook.** Make a clean final copy. Write a title for your story.

**B. Sharing Your Story** Read your story to your class. Draw a picture about your story. Hang the stories and pictures on the bulletin board.

# Speaking and Listening

### Giving a Puppet Show

You can tell a story as a play. One kind of play is a puppet show. In most plays, the actors are people. In a puppet show, the actors are dolls that move.

You can make a puppet out of cardboard attached to a stick. You can also make a puppet from a paper bag, a mitten, or a sock. When you give a puppet show, do these things.

1. Learn what your character says.
2. Learn when it is your turn to speak.
3. Decide what kind of voice your character has. Is your character funny or scary? Change your voice to sound like the character.
4. Speak clearly and loudly enough to be heard.
5. Move your puppet when your character is speaking. Be sure the action follows the story.

### Exercise   Planning and Giving a Puppet Show

Work in groups of three or four. Choose a story for a puppet show. Each person can choose a character to play. Make a puppet of your character.

Practice your puppet show. Follow the guides above. When you are ready, give the show for your class.

# Creative Writing

**A.** Alex wears a Captain Super shirt every day. He says he wears it to feel strong. Write a story about someone who wears something special. Tell what happens when the person wears the clothes. Does the person stay out of trouble? Does the person win something?

**B.** Suzie Serious has a brother who bothers her. She wishes she could snap her fingers and become something else. Sometimes she thinks she would like to be a spider. She could spin a web around herself. Think of another way Suzie could get her wish. Write a story about it.

**C.** Imagine that you live in a lighthouse. One day you are on the beach. You find a bottle floating in the water. There is a message inside the bottle. What is the message? What will you do? Write a story about what happens when you find the message.

# Using English in Social Studies

**Dolphins Save Swimmer's Life**

Can you guess that the sentence above is from a newspaper? Newspaper stories have special titles called **headlines.** The sentence above is a headline for a newspaper story.

Newspapers contain stories about current events. The stories answer these *W* questions.

**Who?   What?   Where?   When?   Why?**

Answers to the *W* questions give all the facts in a story. The headline tells what the story is about.

## Exercise   Writing a Newspaper Story

Think of a current event that would make a good story. Share ideas with your classmates. Choose one idea to write about. Get all the facts. Write the story. Then write a good headline. Here are some ideas for stories.

Pilot Sets New Record
Class President Elected
School Cleanup Day
Circus Train Arrives
Zoo Babies Born

Make a class newspaper of all your stories. Separate the stories into subjects. Some might be about school news. Other stories could be about your neighborhood or city.

# Chapter 10 Review

**A. Learning About Stories** Read this story. Answer the questions that follow.

> My bike picked up speed. Down the hill, faster and faster I went. I squeezed the hand brakes. Nothing happened. I couldn't slow down. I couldn't stop. At that moment I saw three garbage cans. I steered toward them. Bang! clang! Into the cans I crashed! The bike flew one way. I flew another. We both landed safely.

1. Is the character real or make-believe?
2. Where is the setting?
3. Write three things that happen in the bike story.
4. Which of these titles fits the story best?
   a. Collecting Garbage
   b. A Scary Ride
   c. My New Bike

**B. Proofreading Sentences** Read these sentences. Find any run-on sentences or mistakes in capitalization, punctuation, or spelling. Write each sentence correctly.

1. Tillie Troll couldnt sleep.
2. She ate too much her stomach hurt.
3. She stared at the top of hir cave?
4. She counted the bats hanging their.
5. Then tillie troll fell asleep.

# Cumulative Review    Unit 2

## Composition

**Writing a Story**  Write a paragraph about something you did that was fun. Did you ever go on a trip? Have you ever taken an exciting ride? Start by telling who was there and where it happened. Tell about the events in the order they happened. Write a good ending.

## Grammar

**A. Nouns and Pronouns**  Each sentence below has two mistakes in it. Look at all of the nouns, pronouns, and possessive forms to find the mistakes. Write each sentence correctly.

1. Kathy and jane wanted to ride with Miguel and I.
2. They're ship landed at plymouth Rock.
3. The tribes doctor knows how to make medicine from Plants.
4. Him and I washed all of you're dishes.
5. Its in the cage with the three mouses.
6. Alison and them got lost on there way.
7. Me and Gary have collected nine players autographs.
8. That little gray Cat is always chasing it's tail.
9. Two mans carried the heavy boxs up the stairs.
10. Mel stayed home to take care of Beths puppys.

**B. Verbs** Each sentence below has a mistake in the way the verb, contraction, or negative is used. Write each sentence correctly.

1. Sailors gets directions from the stars.
2. We've went to batting practice twice.
3. Ill tell you the answer when you are done.
4. Arthur rips his shirt yesterday.
5. They were never at no museums.
6. Ken always watch the planes take off.
7. You shouldn't never swim alone.
8. The train has arrive in the station.
9. The bees is making honey.
10. Wendy hasn't ate any popcorn.

## Related Skills

**Understanding Stories** Read this story and answer the questions that follow.

> Prairie Patsy was as fast as lightning. Pioneer folks in Illinois say Patsy once sewed a quilt in five minutes. People still talk about the blizzard of 1828. Patsy cleared the road to town by making a ton of snow ice cream.

1. Is this story a fable or a tall tale?
2. Who is the main character?
3. When does the story take place?
4. Where does the story take place?
5. Write another sentence that fits the story.

# UNIT 3

| Chapter 11 | **Learning About Adjectives and Adverbs** |
| Chapter 12 | **Writing a Description** |
| Chapter 13 | **Discovering Poetry** |
| Chapter 14 | **Giving and Following Directions** |
| Chapter 15 | **Writing To Explain How** |

## Sharing Secrets

Unit 3 will help you describe the world around you. You will explore ways to share your ideas about the world by using both facts and your imagination.

You will study adjectives and adverbs. You will use what you learn to write clear explanations, colorful descriptions, and poetry. You will learn how important it is to give and follow directions carefully.

These skills will help you both in and out of school. You can use them to tell how to play a game or how to do a science experiment. You will learn skills that will help you when you take a test. You will learn how to describe all of the things you see, hear, and feel.

The more you learn, the more you will be able to reach out into the world. You can gather your special experiences close to you. Then you can let them go free again for others to see.

## SECRET HAND

I closed my eyes
and made a fist of my hand:

I held a stripe
from the tiger tree,
an emerald snowflake,
a drop of orange rain,
and thirteen purple
grains of sand.

Then
I opened my fingers
and I let them
fly free.

—EVE MERRIAM

# Chapter 11

# Learning About Adjectives and Adverbs

Have you ever been on a merry-go-round? One animal may be *big* and *white*. One may be *small* and *brown*. We use different words to describe each animal. These words are called adjectives.

When you rode on a merry-go-round, how did it move? Did it move *slowly*? *Slowly* tells something about the verb *move*. It tells *how* the merry-go-round moved. *Slowly* is an adverb.

In this chapter, you will learn about adjectives and adverbs. You will see how they make your writing more interesting.

# 1 What Are Adjectives?

> An **adjective** is a word that describes a noun.

Read and compare these sentences.

I saw a big brown bear.
I saw a small black bear.

Which words are different in these sentences? How do these words make you think about different kinds of bears?

The words that are different in each sentence are called adjectives. **Adjectives** are words that describe nouns. That means they tell more about the nouns.

The adjectives *big* and *brown* describe the noun *bear* in one sentence. In the other sentence, the adjectives *small* and *black* describe the bear. Notice how they change the meaning of the sentences.

You can use an adjective before the noun it describes. You can also use an adjective after the noun it describes.

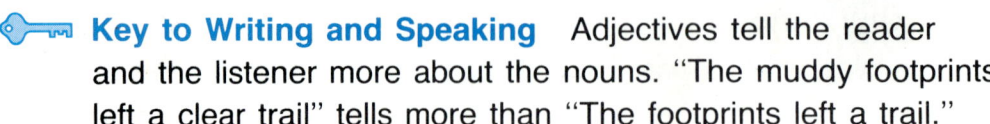

The bear has *brown* fur. (before)
The bear's fur is *brown*. (after)

🔑 **Key to Writing and Speaking** Adjectives tell the reader and the listener more about the nouns. "The muddy footprints left a clear trail" tells more than "The footprints left a trail."

174

## Exercises  Understanding Adjectives

**A.** Write the following sentences. Underline every adjective. Draw an arrow from the adjective to the noun it tells about.

Example: Darnell found a silver key.

1. Peacocks have beautiful tails.
2. Mrs. Logan told us about white elephants.
3. Spiderman climbs tall buildings.
4. Small rocks circle the garden.
5. Cotton is soft.
6. The bedroom is purple.
7. Bulls have sharp horns.
8. My sister writes funny poems.
9. The audience shouted a loud cheer.
10. A new family moved in yesterday.

**B.** Think of an adjective to describe each noun below. Then write a sentence using your adjective and the noun.

Example:  bike   red bike

My parents gave me a red bike.

1. puppy
2. giant
3. town
4. story
5. game
6. hair

**C. Speaking and Listening** Form groups of three or four. Take turns pointing to an object in the room. One person names the noun. The others in the group each tell one adjective to describe that object.

## 2 Kinds of Adjectives

> Adjectives can tell **what kind, how many,** or **which ones.**

In part 1 you learned that adjectives tell **what kind** of thing the noun is. Adjectives can also tell **how many** and **which ones.**

### Adjectives That Tell What Kind

Many adjectives tell **what kind** of person or thing the noun is. Here are some examples.

    noisy    large    yellow    sleepy

    Grandmother likes the *noisy* birds.

Notice that *noisy* and *sleepy* both end in -*y*. Many adjectives that tell *what kind* end in -*y*.

### Adjectives That Tell How Many

Number words are adjectives that tell **how many.**

    one    two    twenty    fifty

    *One* cardinal sat on a branch.

Other adjectives that tell *how many* do not tell exact numbers. Here are some examples.

    some    many    more    several

    *Many* trees grow in the orchard.

## Adjectives That Tell Which Ones

Some adjectives point out nouns. *This, that, these,* and *those* are adjectives that tell **which ones**.

1. Use *this* and *that* with singular nouns.

   this bird     that bird

2. Use *these* and *those* with plural nouns.

   these birds     those birds

*This* and *these* tell about things that are close. *That* and *those* tell about things that are farther away.

Never use *them* as an adjective. It is a pronoun. It stands for a noun. It does not point out a noun.

   Wrong: Feed them birds.
   Right: Feed those birds.

**Key to Writing**  When you write, you often use adjectives to tell what color. There are many color words to choose from. For example, *yellow* can be *lemon* or *gold*. Look at the list of color words in the Word Bank for Writers. You will find different names for colors to use in your writing.

### Exercises  Understanding Adjectives

**A.** Find all of the adjectives in the sentences below. Write the sentences. Underline every adjective. Draw an arrow from the adjective to the noun it tells about.

1. These rockets are launched by big computers.
2. Eskimos build snowhouses in one hour.
3. Many knights wore shiny armor.
4. One diver found several anchors.
5. Most tigers live for twenty years.
6. This little rock has purple spots.
7. Some trains need two engines.
8. That kangaroo has one baby.
9. Forty bikes entered that race.
10. Those pigeons flew fifteen miles.

**B.** Read the following sentences. Choose the correct adjective for each sentence.

1. The divers discovered (that, these) sunken ship.
2. (These, Those) kittens won't get off my lap.
3. (This, That) planet is millions of miles away.
4. Please hand me (those, them) other paddles.
5. (Them, Those) robins didn't come back.

**C. Writing** Some divers find a buried treasure chest. You are there when it is opened. Write about the things inside the chest. Use adjectives to describe the treasures.

# 3 Using *A, An,* and *The*

> The words **a, an,** and **the** are adjectives. There are special rules for their use.

Follow these rules when you use *a, an,* and *the.*

1. **Use *the* before singular or plural nouns.**
    *the* parrot     *the* parrots

2. **Use *a* or *an* before singular nouns only.**
    *a* friend     *an* enemy

3. **Use *a* before words beginning with consonant sounds.**
    *a* hawk     *a* brown owl

4. **Use *an* before words beginning with vowel sounds.**
    *an* owl     *an* angry hawk

## Exercise   Using *A, An,* and *The*

Read each sentence aloud. Use **a** or **an** in the blank.

1. Lightfeather is _____ Iroquois chief.
2. My aunt dropped _____ earring.
3. A spider is _____ useful insect.
4. Mrs. Warren runs _____ day care center.
5. _____ icicle fell from the roof.
6. The hikers spotted _____ raccoon.
7. Beth went up in _____ helicopter.
8. Andy climbed _____ oak tree.
9. The cub got _____ thorn in its paw.
10. It was _____ honor to meet the Senator.

# 4 Using Adjectives To Compare

> When you compare two people or things, you usually add **-er** to the adjective. When you compare three or more people or things, you usually add **-est**.

Adjectives can be used to compare people or things. We can tell how things are alike and how they are different.

## Comparing Two People or Things

These sentences compare a car and a train.

> A car is fast.
> A train is faster than a car.

The first sentence is only about a car. We use the adjective *fast*. The second sentence is about two things, a car and a train. It tells how the two things are different. We add the *-er* ending to *fast* and form the word *faster*.

Some adjectives change their spelling when -er is added. Use these rules for adding -er to those words.

**1. If a word ends in a single consonant following a single vowel, double the final consonant before adding the ending.**

hot + er = hotter

**2. If a word ends in a silent e, drop the final e before adding the ending.**

nic**e** + er = nicer

**3. If a word ends in y following a consonant, change the y to i before adding the ending.**

pretty + er = prettier

## Comparing Three or More People or Things

We can compare the car and the train with a third thing. Read these sentences.

A train is faster than a car.
An airplane is faster than a train.
An airplane is the fastest of all three.

The third sentence compares three things. We added the -est ending to the adjective *fast* to form the word *fastest*. Follow the same spelling rules as when you added -er.

| | | | |
|---|---|---|---|
| **Rule 1** | hot | hotter | hottest |
| **Rule 2** | nice | nicer | nicest |
| **Rule 3** | pretty | prettier | prettiest |

## Exercises  Using -er and -est

**A.** Write each adjective. Then write the **-er** and **-est** forms.

1. hard
2. thin
3. wise
4. fat
5. safe
6. sunny
7. brave
8. old
9. sad
10. lucky

**B.** Choose the correct adjective. Write each sentence correctly.

1. Chan can jump (farther, farthest) than Toby.
2. A gorilla is the (stronger, strongest) of all apes.
3. The (friendlier, friendliest) dog in the neighborhood is Coco.
4. Alicia's score is (higher, highest) than mine.
5. This panda is the (cuter, cutest) in the store.
6. Donna runs (faster, fastest) than Kiru runs.
7. Asia is the (larger, largest) of the seven continents.
8. A whale shark is (bigger, biggest) than an elephant.
9. That fish line sank (deeper, deepest) than the first one.
10. Meg is the (older, oldest) of my three sisters.

**C. Writing** You and two friends visit an apple orchard. Each of you picks the best apple you can find. Write about the three apples. Compare how big they are, how they look, and how they taste.

## 5 What Are Adverbs?

> An **adverb** is a word that describes a verb. It tells **how**, **where**, or **when**. Many adverbs end with *-ly*.

Read this sentence.

Kevin runs.

The verb *runs* tells what Kevin is doing. It does not tell any more. To tell more, you need more words.

Kevin runs quickly.
Kevin runs outside.
Kevin runs often.

Each sentence has a new word that describes the verb *runs*. The word *quickly* tells **how** Kevin runs. The word *outside* tells **where** Kevin runs. The word *often* tells **when** Kevin runs.

The three words are adverbs. **Adverbs** are words that describe, or tell about, verbs. Adverbs tell **how**, **where**, or **when**.

Find the adverbs in these sentences. Decide if they tell *how*, *where*, or *when*.

Irene sings there.
Irene sings loudly.
Irene sings sometimes.

## Adding -ly to Adjectives

Many adverbs are formed by adding *-ly* to an adjective.

| Adjective | + | ly | = | Adverb |
|---|---|---|---|---|
| slow | + | ly | = | slowly |
| safe | + | ly | = | safely |
| easy | + | ly | = | easily |

Sarah speaks *slowly*.
Arturo arrived *safely*.
Carla finished *easily*.

The following chart shows other words that are used often as adverbs.

| How | Where | When |
|---|---|---|
| sadly | up | now |
| softly | down | then |
| gently | away | soon |
| brightly | here | often |
| suddenly | inside | never |
| silently | outside | sometimes |

*Now* the cat creeps *silently away*.

**Exercises**  **Finding and Using Adverbs**

**A.** Write the two headings **Adverbs** and **Verbs.** Find the adverb in each sentence. Write the adverb under the correct heading. Then write the verb it tells about.

1. The pigs squealed loudly.
2. Autumn arrives soon.
3. Katrina looked everywhere for her watch.
4. Chad camped outside with a friend.
5. The beetle crawled slowly.
6. Alonzo never got a library card.
7. The pitcher threw the ball far.
8. My balloon popped suddenly.
9. Robin's father came to class yesterday.
10. The bus driver smiled brightly.

**B.** Choose an adverb from the chart on page 184 to complete each sentence. Write the sentences.

1. Lisa _____ tells a lie.
2. Isaac rode the elevator _____.
3. The lamb followed Erin _____.
4. Our teacher _____ left.
5. My grandmother will arrive _____.
6. The spaceship door opened _____.
7. Sondra _____ waters the plants.
8. The ice cracked _____.
9. Your gerbil lives _____.
10. Mr. Flint _____ returned our rake.

**C. Writing** It is the last race at the picnic. Write an exciting finish. Use adverbs to tell about the action.

185

# Exercises for Mastery  Chapter 11

## Learning About Adjectives and Adverbs

**A. Finding Adjectives** Make two headings on your paper, **Adjectives** and **Nouns.** Write the adjectives from these sentences under the correct heading. Then write the nouns they tell about.

1. Loud noises can break that glass.
2. Martha found three shiny quarters.
3. This ship carries small planes.
4. These new boots are comfortable.
5. Some baboons live on high cliffs.
6. Both teams have several extra players.
7. Many children skate on this icy field.
8. That sly fox caught two chickens.
9. Roberto likes crunchy peanuts.
10. Those silver tops spin on thick rugs.

**B. Using A and An** Read these sentences. Decide if **a** or **an** should be used in each blank space. Write the sentences correctly.

1. Luke can play _____ drum.
2. How many arms does _____ octopus have?
3. The seal leaped through _____ hoop.
4. Some money was found in _____ old trunk.
5. _____ ermine grows white fur in the winter.
6. Tina wants to be _____ airline pilot.
7. I have _____ itch on my nose.
8. Samuel wears _____ pair of gym shoes.
9. Aunt Molly is knitting _____ sweater.
10. _____ alligator can be dangerous.

**C. Using Adjectives To Compare** Choose the correct adjective in each sentence. Say the sentences. Then write them correctly.

1. Jessica wore the (scarier, scariest) of the three masks.
2. A horse has (shorter, shortest) ears than a mule.
3. Geese are the (noisier, noisiest) birds on this farm.
4. The (funnier, funniest) of the three clowns is the hobo.
5. Hummingbirds are the (tinier, tiniest) birds we have.

**D. Finding Adverbs** Write **Adverbs** and **Verbs** on your paper. Write the adverbs under the correct heading. Then write the verbs that the adverbs tell about.

1. Omar polishes his bicycle often.
2. The lizard changed color slowly.
3. Lana beat the drum loudly.
4. The hot air balloon soared up.
5. One sailor spotted a whale yesterday.
6. This glue sticks tightly.
7. A family of wolves lives there.
8. The detective solved the mystery quickly.
9. Alan found a rabbit hole nearby.
10. The lion stretched lazily.

# Using Grammar in Writing

**A.** There is a special zoo for imaginary animals. Make up one animal for this zoo. Write about it. Tell the animal's name. Describe what it looks like. Tell what to feed it and how to care for it. Use adjectives and adverbs to make your writing clear.

**B.** Design a costume for a super hero. Write a paragraph about the costume. Be sure to use words telling color, size, and shape. Use the Word Bank for Writers in the **Power Handbook** to help you choose adjectives. When you are finished writing your paragraph, draw a picture of your super hero.

**C. Using Adjectives and Adverbs in Science** The nine planets in our solar system are listed below. Choose at least three planets. Write sentences to compare them in size to each other. Use an encyclopedia or a science book for help.

| Mercury | Mars    | Uranus  |
|---------|---------|---------|
| Venus   | Jupiter | Neptune |
| Earth   | Saturn  | Pluto   |

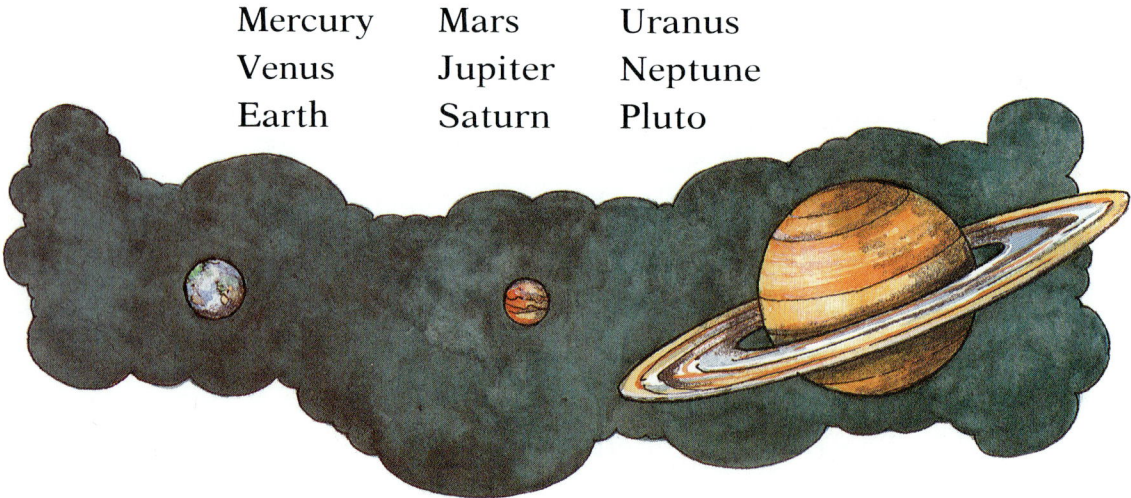

# Chapter 11 Review

**A. Finding Adjectives and Adverbs** Write these headings, **Adjectives** and **Adverbs.** Find one adjective and one adverb in each sentence. Write them under the correct headings. Do not list *a, an,* or *the.*

1. Jana whispered softly to the little kitten.
2. Many flowers bloomed inside.
3. Umpires often wear striped shirts.
4. The long trail ended here.
5. Vincent flipped one coin quickly.
6. The green snake crawled slowly.
7. Elephants usually have ivory tusks.
8. The large engine roared loudly.
9. Paul worked two puzzles easily.
10. The new chicks hatched yesterday.

**B. Using Adjectives Correctly** Choose the correct adjective in each sentence. Write the sentences.

1. (This, That) monkey in the corner is silly.
2. Greg's box is (lighter, lightest) than Meryl's.
3. (Them, Those) vikings wore helmets.
4. Mel's kite went (higher, highest) than Dan's.
5. Indira found (a, an) egg under the bush.
6. The black horse is the (prettier, prettiest) of the three horses.
7. I saw (these, those) clowns in the parade.
8. Val hit the ball (farther, farthest) than Lisa.
9. Rod wore (a, an) uniform for the scouts.
10. Giraffes have the (longer, longest) necks of all the animals.

# Chapter 12

# Writing a Description

Picture a dog in your mind. Is the dog big or small, thin or fat? What color is its fur? Is the fur long or short? Are the dog's ears pointed or floppy? Does the dog have a long or short tail?

When you answer these questions, you are telling how the dog looks. You are describing the dog.

You often need to describe a person, place, or thing. When you write a story, you tell what people and places look like. In science class, you describe plants and animals. You describe a toy you want for your birthday.

In this chapter, you will learn to describe people and things. You will discover how to use words to make a picture in your reader's mind.

# 1 Thinking About Describing

> A description can tell how something looks.

You can help a reader "see" what you see by describing it. You can also share a picture you imagine by describing it. For example, suppose your teacher reads an article about Mars to the class. Your teacher asks you to imagine and describe a Martian. What would you write?

**Read and Think.** Doreen used her imagination. She wrote this description. Try to picture her Martian in your mind as you read.

The Martian looks like a little green man. Two long antennas spring out of its bald head. Its round eyes are blinking red lights. Its nose looks like a doorknob. When its mouth opens, you see a black hole and hear loud squeaks.

**Think and Discuss.** Read Doreen's description again. Look for describing words. Discuss these questions.

1. The paragraph describes parts of the Martian's face. In what order are they described?
2. What colors and shapes does Doreen use?
3. What words describe something you hear?
4. If you drew a picture of the Martian, what would you include?

**Read and Think.** Often a description is part of a story. Read this paragraph from a story about a frog.

> The old bullfrog squatted on a rock. He was taking a sunbath. He was a giant water frog. He had webbed feet for swimming. A short while ago he had shed his skin. Now his new green coat was tight and shiny. The sun felt good on his new skin.
>
> —BERNIECE FRESCHET

**Think and Discuss.** Reread the paragraph. Discuss these questions with your class.

1. What word tells the size of the frog?
2. What word tells the shape of his feet?
3. What words describe his coat?

## Now It's Your Turn

You have read two descriptions. Both described size, shape, and color. Both used describing words and phrases to help you see a picture in your mind. Now you will learn to write a description. You will draw a picture with words.

## 2 Planning and Writing a Description

> To plan a description, picture the person or thing in your mind. Then list the words that describe it.

Follow these steps to begin writing a description.

**1. Choose a subject to describe.** Description is often part of a longer piece of writing. You might be describing a person or place in a story, for example. You can choose a real or an imaginary subject. Choose something you will enjoy writing about.

**2. List describing words.** You can describe something more easily when you look at it. If you can, find a picture of your subject. If your subject is imaginary, draw a picture first.

Three kinds of words tell how something looks. You can use **color** words, **size** words, and **shape** words to describe your subject. The **Power Handbook** lists color, size, and shape words on page 342.

Jeff decided to describe a nest on the branch of a tree. First, he made notes about how it looked. He wrote words to describe its color, size, and shape.

| Color | Size | Shape |
|---|---|---|
| green leaves | tiny flowers | pointed leaves |
| pink flowers | small egg | round nest |
| brown straw | thin crack | oval egg |

**3. Write a topic sentence.** Your first sentence should tell what you are describing. Read Jeff's topic sentence.

I can see a bird's nest on a branch of my tree.

**4. Write a draft that describes your person or thing.** Write three or four sentences that include words from your list. Try to describe your subject in the order you might look at it. For example, you could describe it from outside to inside or top to bottom.

## Exercise   Prewriting and Writing a Description

Think of a person, place, or thing you want to describe. Look at page 334 in the **Power Handbook** for ideas. Find a picture of your subject. Make a list of words that describe it.

Begin writing your draft. Write a topic sentence. Then write several other sentences that describe the subject. Use your list of words as you write the sentences.

## 3 Revising and Sharing a Description

> Revise your description to make it better.
> Proofread it for mistakes. Then copy it neatly.

Read your description again. Does it give you a clear picture in your mind? Can you think of words to help your reader "see" it better?

Use these guides to make your word pictures as clear as you can.

### Guides for Revising

1. Should I add any color, shape, or size words?
2. Can I add words to describe the sound, smell, feel, or taste of my subject?
3. Have I described my subject in a good order?

Read the draft of Jeff's description. Then look at the changes he made. Jeff's thoughts as he revised are shown in blue.

*(I need size and color words.)*

*(I can describe the egg better.)*

I can see a bird's nest on a ^large branch of my tree. It rests among ^pointed green leaves and ^tiny pink flowers. A small ^oval egg lies inside the nest. The nest is a circle of dry ^brown straw. I can see a ^thin crack on the smooth ^blue shell.

*(I should change the order.)*

Now you can proofread your draft. Look for mistakes in the use of capital letters. Check your punctuation and spelling. Use proofreading marks from page 331 to correct your mistakes. Copy your description in your best handwriting.

Read the final copy of Jeff's description. Notice that Jeff added size, shape, and color words as he revised. He also changed the order of two sentences. Why does that change make sense?

> I can see a bird's nest on a large branch of my tree. It rests among pointed green leaves and tiny pink flowers. The nest is a circle of dry brown straw. A small oval egg lies inside the nest. I can see a thin crack on the smooth blue shell.

## Exercises  Finishing and Sharing a Description

**A. Revising Your Paragraph** Revise your description to make a better word picture. Then proofread your paragraph. Correct mistakes in capital letters, punctuation, and spelling. Finally, copy your paragraph in your neatest handwriting.

**B. Sharing Your Paragraph** You have written a good word picture to describe your topic. Now draw a picture to go with your description. Use the colors and shapes your paragraph describes. Prepare to share your picture and description with others. Put in on the bulletin board or make a booklet with the class.

# Speaking and Listening

## Listening for Sounds

You have been describing a person, place, or thing. You can also describe sounds. Even when it seems quiet, you hear sounds. You hear the wind blowing, floors creaking, pencils scratching. When you listen carefully, you can figure out the sounds.

Some of the nicest sounds are the sounds of music. If you listen carefully, you can hear different instruments or voice parts. You may hear changes in the music. Listen for fast or slow parts, loud or soft parts. Listen for the mood, or feeling, the music gives. Is the mood happy, sad, or playful? As you listen, think of words to describe what you hear and feel. Here are examples of words you might use: *jumpy, booming, spooky, exciting, cheerful.*

## Exercise  Listening to Music

Listen to music in class. As you listen, write down words that describe what you hear. Think about how the music makes you feel.

When you have listed words to describe the music, talk about it in class. Find out if others heard things you missed. Compare your feelings about the music with others. Then listen to the music again. Did other people's ears wake you up to new sounds?

# Creative Writing

**A.** Imagine that you are invited to a very unusual dinner. Before you can eat, your eyes are covered. You can use only your hands, nose, and mouth to figure out what you are eating. Write a paragraph that describes how one kind of food feels, smells, and tastes.

**B.** What kind of toy could a giant play with? Describe what the toy might look like. You may want to use some size words from the Word Bank for Writers. Look at page 342 in the **Power Handbook.**

**C.** Pretend that you have a magic paintbrush. This paintbrush can change the colors of anything outside. The colors change in an instant. Touch the paintbrush to something outside. Describe how the thing looks now.

# Using English in Science

There are many ways to describe something. Scientists often use **diagrams.** These are pictures that show the parts of an object with labels.

Look at this diagram of a tree. Read the labels.

## Exercise  Making a Diagram

Think of something that you can make a diagram of. It should be a plant or an animal. Make a sketch of your subject, or cut out a picture of it. Draw lines out from each part. Write a label for each part.

Now, write a paragraph that describes your subject. Put your diagram and paragraph together. Share your complete description with your class.

# Chapter 12 Review

**A. Thinking About a Description** Read this description. Then answer the questions below.

> Duchess is a raccoon. She has a pointed nose and small eyes. The black fur around her eyes looks like a mask. Her ears are triangles rising from her head. Brown fur covers her chubby body. Rings of yellow and dark brown circle her tail. Her short legs end in paws that look like fingers. She uses her front paws like hands to wash her food. Then she pops it into her mouth.

1. Which sentence tells what the description is about?
2. What are three words that describe shape?
3. What are three words that describe color?
4. Which two words describe size?
5. What does the writer compare the raccoon's paws to?

**B. Using Words That Describe** Rewrite the sentences. Add words that tell color, shape, or size.

1. The _____ light blinked on and off.
2. A _____ snake wiggled in the _____ grass.
3. _____ clouds appeared in the _____ sky.
4. A _____ fish swam toward the _____ rock.
5. The lady's hat was _____ and _____.

201

# Chapter 13

# Discovering Poetry

Poems are full of beauty and mystery. Poems grow and change as you read them. The more you read a poem, the more it says to you.

Poems express feelings. Poems can put a picture in your mind. They can also help you hear sounds. What do you feel, see, and hear in this poem?

### Hokku
In the falling snow
A laughing boy holds out his palms
Until they are white.
—RICHARD WRIGHT

In this chapter, you will read and enjoy several poems. You will discover how poets use words to create pictures, sounds, and feelings.

# 1 What Is a Poem?

> A poem is a group of words put together in a special way. Poems can express feelings.

A poem is a special kind of writing. It tells an idea in a few words. This idea may be a picture or a feeling. Each word in the poem adds to the idea.

A poem is written differently from a paragraph. Poets write in **lines.** These lines may or may not be sentences. The lines are grouped into **stanzas.**

Poems are often written to show common things in new or unusual ways. To do this, poets use their imagination. Read this poem. It has two stanzas.

### City

In the morning the city
Spreads its wings
Making a song
In stone that sings.

In the evening the city
Goes to bed
Hanging lights
About its head.
—LANGSTON HUGHES

In the first stanza, the poet describes the city in the morning. He compares the city to a bird that makes a song. In this way, he changes a common sight into something very special.

The second stanza tells about the city at night. In the poem, the city goes to bed like a person. What are the lights around its head? What kind of feeling does the second stanza give you?

Poems come in many shapes and sizes. Some poems have only one stanza. Read this poem that gives an idea in only a few words. The poet reminds us that time changes even a large, hard rock into a handful of sand.

### Rocks

Big rocks into pebbles,
pebbles into sand,
I really held a million million rocks here
  in my hand.
—FLORENCE PARRY HEIDE

## Exercise  Thinking About a Poem

Read the following poem. Discuss the answers to the questions with your classmates.

### Spring

When you see a daffodil
and know it's spring,
all the songs inside of you
begin to sing.
—AILEEN FISHER

1. How many stanzas does this poem have?
2. What picture does the poet use for spring?
3. How do you feel when spring arrives?

## 2 Seeing Pictures in a Poem

> A poem can paint a picture in the reader's mind.

You have seen that poets help you look at things in a new way. Poets compare different things to put a picture in your mind. They choose words carefully to describe sights, sounds, tastes, and smells. They try to give you a new feeling about something.

Read this poem about stormy days. What new picture comes to your mind?

### Brooms

On stormy days
When the wind is high
Tall trees are brooms
Sweeping the sky.

They swish their branches
In buckets of rain,
And swash and sweep it
Blue again.
—DOROTHY ALDIS

Have you ever thought about trees looking like brooms? Do you think this idea is a good one? Were you able to see the trees sweeping the sky?

Read the poem at the top of page 207. What animal does the poet compare fog to? Does this idea help you think about fog in a new way?

### Fog

The fog comes
  on little cat feet.
It sits looking
over harbor and city
on silent haunches
and then moves on.
—CARL SANDBURG

## Exercises   Seeing Pictures in a Poem

**A.** Read this poem. Answer the questions below.

### Clouds

White sheep, white sheep
On a blue hill,
When the wind stops
You all stand still.
When the wind blows
You walk away slow.
White sheep, white sheep,
Where do you go?
  —CHRISTINA G. ROSSETTI

1. What are the clouds being compared to?
2. What is the "blue hill"?
3. When are the "animals" still?
4. How do the "animals" finally move?
5. What feeling do you get from this poem?

**B.** Use your imagination. Write a short poem about an ordinary thing. Try to show the ordinary thing in a new or unusual way. You might use one of these ideas.

Bug    Pencil    Leaf    Car

## 3 Hearing the Sounds in a Poem

> Sounds add meaning to poems. Read poems aloud to hear the sounds of the words and letters.

The sounds of letters and words add meaning to a poem. Read every poem aloud. Listen for these special uses of sound: rhyming words, echoic words, and repeating sounds.

**Rhyming Words** Words that rhyme have the same sound. *Hot* and *lot* rhyme. *Wiggle* and *giggle* rhyme.

**Echoic Words** Echoic words sound like what they mean. *Hum* and *crackle* are echoic words.

Read this poem aloud. Listen for rhyming words and echoic words. Listen for the sounds of the band.

### Here Comes the Band

The band comes booming down the street
The tuba oomphs, the flutes tweet tweet;
The trombones slide, the trumpets blare,
The baton twirls up in the air.
   There's "ooh's!" and "ah's!" and cheers and clapping—
And I can't stop my feet from tapping.
                    —WILLIAM COLE

Each pair of lines in the poem rhymes. *Street* and *tweet* rhyme. What other words rhyme?

Now look for echoic words. In the first line, the band is *booming*. *Oomph* gives the sound of a tuba. What other sounds do you notice?

**Repeating Sounds** Sometimes poets repeat the same consonant sounds in several words. The sound usually reminds us of what the poem describes.

Listen for repeated sounds in this stanza.

> Galoshes
>
> Susie's galoshes
> Make splishes and sploshes
> As Susie steps slowly
> Along in the slush.
> —RHODA BACMEISTER

What do the *s*, *sh*, and *sl* sounds make you think of?

**Exercise   Hearing the Sounds in a Poem**

Read this riddle poem. Then answer the questions below.

> What in the World?
>
> What in the world
>   goes whiskery friskery
>     meowing and prowling
>       napping and lapping
>         at silky milk?
> Psst,
> What is it?
> —EVE MERRIAM

1. What animal is being described?
2. Write three pairs of rhyming words.
3. Write two echoic words the poet used.
4. Do the sounds of this poem remind you of the animal?

## 4 Feeling the Rhythm of a Poem

> Listen for the rhythm, or strong beats, in a poem. The rhythm and meaning of a poem work together.

Many poems have a strong, regular beat. This pattern of strong beats is called **rhythm.** When you read poems aloud, listen for the rhythm. You can tap out the beats as you read or listen. Think about what the poet is saying. Let the rhythm and the meaning work together.

Listen while your teacher reads this poem. The poet has arranged the beats in a pattern. Notice how he captured the rhythm of a swing.

### The Swing

How do you like to go up in a swing,
   Up in the air so blue?
Oh, I do think it the pleasantest thing
   Ever a child can do!

Up in the air and over the wall,
   Till I can see so wide,
Rivers and trees and cattle and all
   Over the countryside—

Till I look down on the garden green,
   Down on the roof so brown—
Up in the air I go flying again,
   Up in the air and down!

—ROBERT LOUIS STEVENSON

Read the first stanza aloud. The strong beats have been marked for you. Tap out those beats as you read. Do you feel the motion of the swing?

How do you like to go úp in a swíng,
  Úp in the aír so blúe?
Óh, I do thínk it the pléasantest thíng
  Éver a chíld can dó!

## Exercises  Feeling the Rhythm of a Poem

**A.** Here's another poem with a strong rhythm. Listen while your teacher reads it aloud. Then see the directions below.

### A Kite

I óften sít and wísh that Í
Could be a kite up in the sky,
And ride upon the breeze and go
Whichever way I chanced to blow.

There are four strong beats in each line. Did you hear them? Copy the poem. Put a mark (/) above each word that has a strong beat. The first line is marked for you.

**B.** Choose a poem with a strong rhythm. Practice reading the poem aloud several times. Then read it to the class.

# Using English in Art

The poem in the picture is in the shape of a caterpillar. It is a concrete poem. A **concrete poem** is one that takes the shape of its subject. The poet writes the lines of the poem to fit the shape of whatever the poem is about. When the poem is finished, it looks like a picture.

A concrete poem can be very short like this one, or much longer. The poem may or may not rhyme.

## Exercise   Writing a Concrete Poem

Write a concrete poem of your own. The following suggestions will help you.

1. First, decide what you want to write about. You might choose a tree or flower, an apple or an animal—anything you wish.

2. Then, think about your subject. Imagine its color, size, and shape. Draw a simple outline shape.

3. Write your poem inside the shape. Make sure your poem tells about the picture.

4. Share your poem with your friends and family.

# Chapter 13 Review

**Thinking About a Poem** Read "Wind Song." Then answer the questions below.

> Wind Song
> When the wind blows
> the quiet things speak.
> Some whisper, some clang,
> Some creak.
>
> Grasses swish.
> Treetops sigh.
> Flags slap
> and snap at the sky.
> Wires on poles
> whistle and hum.
> Ashcans roll.
> Windows drum.
>
> When the wind goes—
> suddenly
> then,
> the quiet things
> are quiet again. —LILIAN MOORE

1. What is the poem about?
2. What beginning consonant sound is repeated in the first line?
3. What echoic word tells what grasses do? What two words tell what flags do?
4. Write three pairs of rhyming words.
5. What are the "quiet things" in the poem?

# Chapter 14

# Giving and Following Directions

Pretend that you are going to a new school. Someone gives you the wrong directions. You turn right at one corner instead of left. You are lost!

Suppose that you are making popcorn. You add a cup instead of a teaspoon of salt. You did not read the directions carefully. The popcorn tastes terrible!

Directions are very important. Poor directions cause mistakes. Not following directions carefully also causes mistakes. Sometimes these mistakes are funny. Sometimes they cause serious problems.

In this chapter, you will learn how to give clear directions. You will learn to follow both oral and written directions. Read and listen carefully. Your eyes and ears can help you learn!

## 1 Giving Directions to Others

> Give clear directions to help others find places.

Sometimes you need to tell someone how to get somewhere. For example, you may have to tell a friend how to get to your house. Try to make your directions simple. Give the directions one step at a time. Give some details that will help the person.

Tom invited José to play at his house. José had never been to Tom's house before. Read the directions Tom gave José.

1. Go down your street toward the gas station.
2. Turn right at the gas station.
3. Walk three blocks.
4. Turn left onto Ridge Street.
5. My house is the second from the corner. It is on the left side of the street. The front door is red. The number is 205.

Are Tom's directions clear? What special places did he name? What other helpful details did he give to José?

> **Guides for Giving Directions**
>
> 1. Give all the steps in order.
> 2. Name special places and give details.
> 3. Have your listener repeat the steps. Make sure he or she understands them.

## Exercises  Giving Directions to Others

**A.** Look at this map of Miller School.

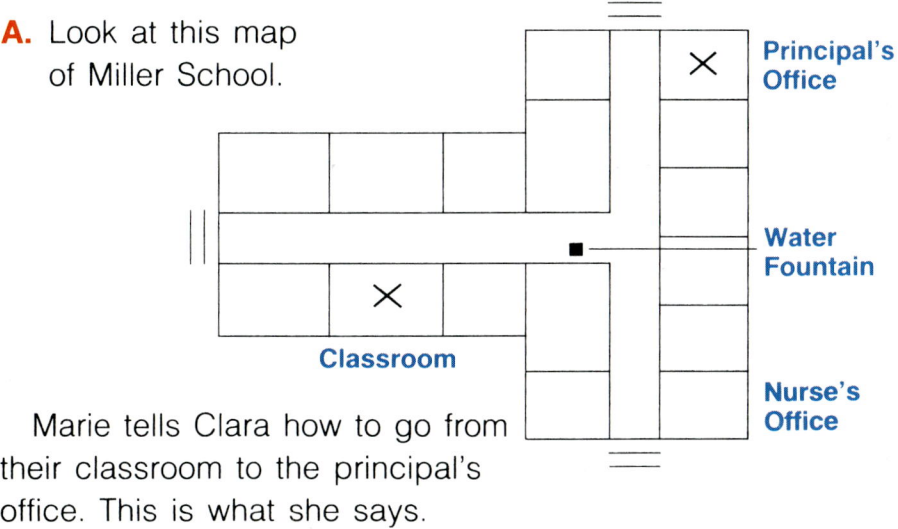

Marie tells Clara how to go from their classroom to the principal's office. This is what she says.

1. Go down the hall.
2. Turn by the water fountain.
3. Go down that hall.
4. The principal's office is next to the stairs.

Why can't Clara follow these directions? Change the directions so she can follow them. Talk about the changes with the rest of your class.

**B.** Give Clara directions to get to the nurse's office from her classroom. Use the map in Exercise A.

# 2  Following Written Directions

> Directions can tell how to do something. Read and follow these directions carefully.

Directions give you information in steps. Often, they explain how to do something. You must read directions carefully *before* you begin. Information you need may show up in later steps.

Follow the steps in the right order. Do not skip any steps. If you don't understand something, ask for help.

Jenny has a book of paper animals. Read the directions that came with her book.

---

Animal Cut-Outs
1. Use sharp scissors to cut out each animal. CAUTION: Always point scissors away from you.
2. Fold the base of the animal along the dotted line.
3. Glue the base of each animal on the cardboard squares.

---

Answer these questions. Talk about your answers.

1. What art supplies does Jenny need?
2. What might happen if Jenny skips step 2?
3. Why should you pay special attention to something marked CAUTION?

> **Guides for Following Written Directions**
>
> 1. Read the directions carefully. Don't skip any steps.
> 2. If you don't understand something, ask for help.
> 3. Pay attention to directions about safety.

## Exercises   Following Written Directions

**A.** Read this set of directions. Then tell the things you would need.

1. Draw a circle on your paper.
2. Color the circle yellow.
3. Cut out the circle.
4. Tape the circle to a blank piece of paper. Make it a sun. Draw a picture around it.

**B.** Read these directions. Then answer the questions below.

---

How To Change a Light Bulb in a Lamp

CAUTION: Unplug the lamp cord first.
1. Unscrew the old light bulb.
2. Take out the old light bulb.
3. Screw in a new light bulb.
4. Plug in the lamp cord.

---

1. What sentence tells about safety?
2. What would happen if you skipped step 1?
3. What would happen if you did step 4 before step 3?

# 3 Listening to Oral Directions

> Listen carefully to oral directions. Ask questions if you do not understand.

Spoken directions are called **oral** directions. You will often be given oral directions in school and at home. Your teacher may explain how to do a math problem or what page of homework to do. Your parents may tell you how to use a new can opener.

You must pay close attention to oral directions. Listen carefully and think about what you are hearing. When you don't understand, ask questions.

Sometimes your teacher tells you how to fill in a form or take a test. For example, Bruce's teacher told the class how to fill out the top of their test forms.

> "Print your name in the little boxes. Write your last name first. Leave a space after your last name. Then, print your first name. Print in capital letters."

Look at these four sets of boxes. Which is correct?

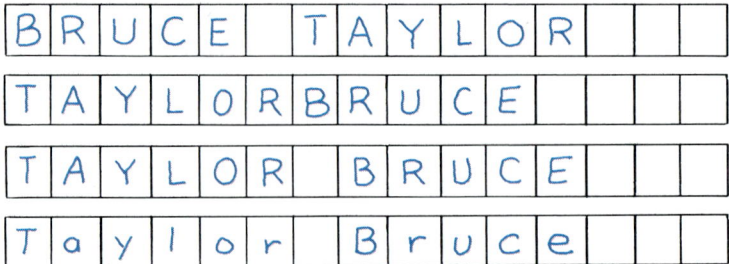

Remember these guides when you listen to directions.

> **Guides for Listening to Directions**
>
> 1. Listen carefully. Do not talk.
> 2. Think about what you are hearing.
> 3. Listen until the directions are finished. Ask questions if you don't understand.

## Exercise  Following Oral Directions

1. Draw three lines and four circles on your paper. Draw them anywhere you want. Don't show your paper to anyone.

2. Choose a partner. Your partner needs a blank paper and pencil. Give your partner directions to draw lines and circles the same way you did.

3. Compare your partner's drawing with your own. How well did your partner follow oral directions? How well did you give them?

4. Now, you be the listener. Follow your partner's oral directions. This time, how well did you both do?

# 4 Following Test Directions

> When you take a test, listen to oral directions. Read written directions carefully.

You need to understand test directions *before* you start a test. Sometimes your teacher gives directions orally. Sometimes you read the directions.

Test directions tell how to mark the answers. Some test directions say to write a word in the blank. Some say to fill in a shape or circle the answer. Others ask you to write the letter of the answer.

Read or listen carefully to the directions for each test you take. You might know the correct answer. If you do not mark it correctly, however, your answer will be wrong.

Read the directions for this test. Which answer is marked correctly?

| Directions: Choose the best word for each sentence. Fill in the circle of the correct answer. |
|---|
| Carol was smiling because she was _____.     A. angry ○ <br>     B. (happy) ○ <br>     C. hurt ○ |
| Carol was smiling because she was _____.     A. angry ○ <br>     B. happy ● <br>     C. hurt ○ |

## Exercises  Following Test Directions

**A.** Read these test directions. Which student marked the answer correctly?

> Directions: One word in the list means the same as the underlined word. Circle the letter of that word.

**Marla**

1. repair    A̶. fix
    B. break
    C. buy

**Dana**

1. repair    A. (fix)
    B. break
    C. buy

**Ross**

1. repair    (A) fix
    B. break
    C. buy

**Ivan**

1. repair    A. fix
    B. break
    C. buy

**B.** First, read these test directions. Then answer the questions below.

> Directions: Find the misspelled word in each list below. Fill in the circle next to the word.

1. In this test, do you write any words?
2. How many words are misspelled in each list?
3. How should you mark the answer?

# Using English in Health and Safety

In an emergency, you must listen carefully to directions. Think clearly and follow directions quickly. Remember safety rules. Your listening and thinking skills can save you from getting hurt.

## Exercise   Following Safety Directions

Read this description of a school fire drill. Decide what is wrong. Then discuss the questions below it.

A loud buzzer sounds in the hall.

MR. PARK: That's a fire alarm. Stop talking. Line up at the door. Follow Lee out of the room. Leave your coats.

MAX: Wait for me, Sara. I need my jacket.

SARA: Okay, Max. I'll wait here.

The rest of the class walks down the hall. Max goes to his locker for his jacket. Sara waits in the room. Max comes back to the room. The class is gone. The building is empty except for Sara and Max.

1. What directions did Max's teacher give?
2. What did Max do that was wrong? What could happen to Max and Sara if there were a fire?
3. Why do schools have fire drills?
4. Make a list of safety rules of your school. Talk about why these rules were made.

# Chapter 14 Review

**A. Giving Directions** Pretend that a new student joined your class today. Write directions for the new student to go from your classroom to the school library.

**B. Following Written Directions** Read these directions. Then answer the questions that follow.

> How To Make a Sandwich
> 1. Get two slices of bread.
> 2. Put lettuce on one slice.
> 3. Put cheese or meat on top of the lettuce.
> 4. Put the second slice of bread on top of the other parts.
> 5. Cut the sandwich in half. Be sure to keep your fingers away from the sharp edge of the knife.

1. What do you need to follow these directions?
2. Which is the direction about safety?
3. What would happen if you skipped step 4?

**C. Following Test Directions** Read these test directions. Then follow them.

> Directions: Copy these words on your paper. Underline the one that does not rhyme with <u>boat</u>.
> 
> coat    wrote    vote    beat

# Chapter 15

# Writing To Explain How

How does a rocket work? How do you make soap? How do you play touchball? We often want to know how to do or make something. We want the directions to be complete and easy to follow.

We learn many things by following directions. It is important that the directions be clear. It is also important to learn how to give clear directions. There are many times when we must tell others *how* to do something.

In this chapter, you will learn about writing to tell how. You will learn a process of writing that will help you explain things to others.

# 1 Thinking About Explaining How

> A paragraph may explain how to do or make something.

Sometimes you need to write a paragraph that explains how to do or make something. Suppose your teacher has asked you to explain how to do an art project. What kind of paragraph would you write?

## Example 1

**Read and Think.** Vickie wrote these directions about how to make a mosaic. A mosaic is a picture made of small stones or other materials.

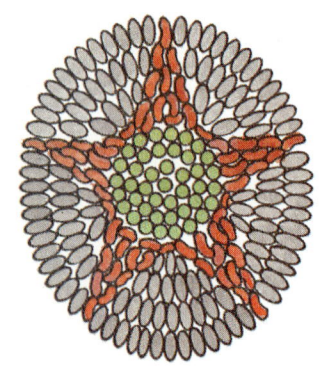

You can make a mosaic out of beans. You will need several colors of dry beans, a piece of cardboard, and glue. First, draw a design on the cardboard. Next, spread glue on a small part. Choose a color for that part. Then, place beans on the glue. Continue spreading glue and filling in each part with other beans. When you are finished, let the glue dry. You will have a beautiful picture.

**Think and Discuss.** Reread Vickie's paragraph. Talk about these questions with your classmates.

1. What is Vickie's topic sentence?
2. What materials do you need to make a mosaic?
3. Does Vickie tell all the steps you must follow?

# Example 2

**Read and Think.** Vickie's paragraph explained how to make something. Here is a paragraph that tells how to do an experiment.

Here is an interesting experiment with sound. Find five empty glasses of the same size. Put a little water in the first glass. Put a little more water in the second glass. Keep filling each of the other glasses a little fuller. The fifth glass should have more water in it than any of the others. Now tap each glass gently with a pencil or a hard stick. Which glass has the highest sound? Which has the lowest sound?
—GERALD CRAIG and BEATRICE DAVIS HURLEY

**Think and Discuss.** Talk about these questions with your class. Look back at the paragraph for help.

1. What is the topic sentence in the paragraph?
2. Are the steps in an order that makes sense?
3. Are the directions easy to follow?
4. Does the picture make the directions clearer?

## Now It's Your Turn

You have read two paragraphs that tell how. The first paragraph explains how to make something. The second tells how to do something. Both give steps in the order they happen. Now you will learn to write a paragraph that tells how.

# 2 Planning and Writing a *How* Paragraph

> Follow these prewriting steps before you write a *how* paragraph. Decide what your paragraph will be about. Make a list of directions in order.

Follow these steps for planning and writing a *how* paragraph.

**1. Choose your topic.** Decide what to write about. First, think about things you know how to do. Can you make a kite? Do you know a good experiment? Have you ever made a puppet?

Perhaps there is something you would like to learn to do. Do you want to learn to make a drum? Look in a craft book that tells how to make drums. Then, try making a drum before you write about it. Remember to choose a topic that is not too big to write about in a paragraph.

**2. Write notes about your topic.** Start by writing your topic as a heading. Then, write a list of the supplies you need. Next, think about the steps you must follow. Write notes about each step in the order it happens. Number your steps.

**3. Write your draft.** Now you are ready to write your draft. Write a topic sentence that tells what you are going to explain. Then, tell any supplies that are needed. Next, use your notes to write a sentence about each step. Write the steps in the order they should be done.

Here are the prewriting notes of a boy named Bernard. He decided to tell how to make a musical instrument.

How to make a musical instrument

1. need two foil pans, beans, and tape
2. put beans in one pan
3. cover with other pan
4. tape pans together

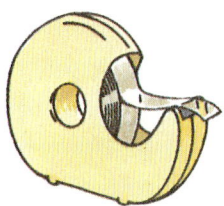  

Now Bernard is ready to write a topic sentence and a draft.

## Exercises Planning and Writing Your *How* Paragraph

**A. Choosing a Topic** Complete each of these sentences three different ways. The six sentences will give you ideas that you can write about.

I know how to _____

I would like to learn how to _____

**B. Writing a Draft** Use one of your ideas from Exercise A to choose a topic. You may also look on page 335 of the **Power Handbook** for ideas. List all the supplies you need. Write notes about your topic as Bernard did above. Next, write a topic sentence telling what your paragraph is about. Then, write a draft from your notes.

231

## 3 Revising and Sharing a *How* Paragraph

> Revise your paragraph to make it clearer. Make a neat, final copy.

**Revising Your Paragraph** Paragraphs that explain how must be easy to follow. Here are some guides.

### Guides for Revising a *How* Paragraph

1. Did you name all the supplies that are needed?
2. Did you include all the steps to be done?
3. Are the steps in an order that makes sense?
4. Are your sentences complete thoughts?
5. Did you check capitalization, punctuation, and spelling?

Bernard asked a friend to read his draft. The friend asked him questions about steps that were not clear. Bernard changed his paragraph to make it clearer.

You can make a musical instrument out of things ^from the kitchen. ^you find. Find two foil pie pans, ^a handful of ~~some~~ dried beans, and a roll of tape. ^First, Put the beans into one pan. ^Next, Put the other pan ^upside down over the first pan. ^Then, Tape the ^edges of the pans together. Now ^you can shake the pans and make some music.

Bernard's friend had asked these questions. Did Bernard's changes answer the questions?

1. Where can I find the things I need?
2. How many beans do I need?
3. How do you put the pans together?

Bernard also added some signal words to help tell the order of the steps. Words like *first, next, then,* and *finally* are signal words. Use a comma after a signal word at the beginning of a sentence.

**Making a Final Copy** Here is Bernard's final copy. He proofread it for mistakes in capital letters, punctuation, and spelling. Then, he was ready to share it with the class.

You can make a musical instrument out of things from the kitchen. Find two foil pie pans, a handful of dried beans, and a roll of tape. First, put the beans into one pan. Next, put the other pan upside down over the first pan. Then, tape the edges of the pans together. Now you can shake the pans and make some music.

## Exercise  Revising and Sharing Your Paragraph

Take out the draft you wrote for part 2. Read it and make changes to make it better. Follow the Guides for Revising a *How* Paragraph. Then, make a clean final copy. Proofread your final copy to be sure you have made all the changes.

Trade paragraphs with a friend. Each of you should see if you can follow what the other person is explaining.

# Speaking and Listening

## Giving a Talk To Tell How

Have you ever told a friend how to play a game? Have you ever shown someone how to do a trick or make a paper hat?

Sometimes you need to give a talk that tells how. You need to tell a group how to do something. Telling how is like writing how. You follow the same steps.

> **Guides for Telling How**
>
> 1. Be prepared. Have your supplies ready.
> 2. Practice the steps in order.
> 3. Speak slowly and clearly. Use notes to help you remember the steps.
> 4. Pause after each step. Invite your audience to ask questions.
> 5. Make sure your audience can see what you are showing and doing.

## Exercise  Telling How To Do or Make Something

Use the paragraph you wrote for this chapter. Gather all the supplies you will need. Learn the steps in the correct order. Plan your talk. Tell your class how to do or make what you wrote about.

Perhaps you wrote about something you cannot do in class. In that case, draw pictures of the steps. Show your audience the pictures as you explain each step.

# Creative Writing

**A.** Not everyone can fly a magic carpet. You must know the secret words. Write a paragraph telling how to make your carpet take off. Tell how to make it turn. Explain how to land it.

**B.** You and a friend are lost on an island. You need to build something to live in. You find some wood, large palm leaves, and vines. There are some large rocks, too. Write how you would build a place to live. Build it so the rain won't come in. Make it safe from wild animals.

**C.** Here is a picture of your new invention. This machine does something that has never been done before. Write about your machine. Tell what it does. Tell how to work the machine. Give the steps in the correct order.

# Using English in Health

The kind of food we eat is important for good health. Our daily diet should include fresh fruits and vegetables. Milk, cheese, and yogurt are also good for us.

We should avoid foods with too much fat or sugar. Some of the foods that are good for us are listed below. They taste good, too! Which ones do you like?

| apples | cheese | peanut butter |
| bread | fruit juice | nuts |
| carrots | granola | popcorn |
| celery | honey | raisins |
| cereal | milk | yogurt |

What healthy, delicious snack could you make from these foods? Could you tell someone how to make your snack? Writing how to make a snack is writing that tells how.

### Exercise   Writing How To Make a Snack

Write directions for making the World's Greatest Snack. Use foods from the list above. Give your snack a delicious-sounding name. List all the things that go into it. Write all the steps to follow. You might try making your snack at home.

# Chapter 15 Review

**A. Understanding Directions** Read the paragraph below. Answer the questions that follow.

> You can make butter from cream. Pour about half a pint of heavy cream into a big bowl. Beat it. First it will turn into whipped cream. Keep on beating. It will change. Part of it will become watery, and part will be little pale yellow lumps. Pour out the water. Spread the rest on bread.
>
> —ALIKI

1. Write the topic sentence of this paragraph.
2. Name the things you need.
3. How do you know when to stop beating the whipped cream?

**B. Using Proofreading Marks** Read this paragraph. Write the paragraph correctly. Follow the changes that are marked.

¶You and your friends can play follow the leader. First, choose a leader. line up behind the ~~the~~ leader. Then, do whatever the leader does. Stop when a player makes a ~~misteak~~ *mistake*. Choose a new ~~L~~eader, *and* start again.

# Cumulative Review

Unit 3

## Composition

**A. Writing a Description** Choose a wild animal. Make a list of words that describe the animal. Write a topic sentence that tells something interesting about it. Use the words in your list for ideas to write other sentences that describe the animal.

**B. Writing To Explain *How*** Write a paragraph telling how to play a game you know. Tell the name of the game and all the things you need to play it. Then tell the rules. Be sure the rules are in the order that the game is played.

## Grammar

**Adjectives and Adverbs** Write the sentences below. Circle the adjective (except *a, an,* or *the*) or adverb in each sentence. Draw a line under the word it tells about.

1. Marla tied those ribbons.
2. Start the engine now.
3. Does the flag have thirteen stripes?
4. The goalie leaped forward.
5. Jan grows the prettiest flowers.
6. William tiptoed quietly.
7. Several hawks appeared.
8. Celia has a black kitten.
9. The jack-in-the-box popped up.
10. This tire needs air.

## Related Skills

**A. Understanding Poetry** Read this poem. Answer the questions that follow.

### The Lizard

The lizard is a timid thing
That cannot dance or fly or sing;
He hunts for bugs beneath the floor
And longs to be a dinosaur.
—JOHN GARDNER

1. What is the poem about?
2. Write the two pairs of rhyming words.
3. Write the first two lines of the poem on your paper. Put a mark (/) above each word that has a strong beat.

**B. Following Directions** Read and follow the test directions below.

> Copy each row of words on your paper. Draw a circle around the word that does not belong in each row.

1. walk    spill    run    skip    jump
2. table   chair    roof   desk    lamp
3. eat     bake     fry    roast   boil

# UNIT 4

| Chapter 16 | **Writing Friendly Letters** |
| Chapter 17 | **Thinking Clearly** |
| Chapter 18 | **Getting To Know the Library** |
| Chapter 19 | **Writing a Report** |
| Chapter 20 | **Using Capital Letters** |
| Chapter 21 | **Using Punctuation Marks** |

## Searching

In Unit 4, you will use all of the skills you have learned. You will use them to search for and share information. You will also sharpen your thinking skills.

You will find out how to share news in a letter. You will learn to find facts in the library. You will use thinking skills to sort out information you gather. In a report, you will be able to pass on what you learn to others.

Clear thinking and writing will help you in all of your subjects. You will write better reports in social studies. You will solve problems in math and science.

What you have learned in this book can carry you on many different paths. Let your curiosity and wonder guide you. Reach out and explore new things. The world is filled with things waiting to be discovered.

## NIGHT

Stars over snow,
    And in the west a planet
Swinging below a star—
    Look for a lovely thing and
    you will find it,
It is not far—
    It never will be far.

—SARA TEASDALE

# Chapter 16

# Writing Friendly Letters

Do you have friends who live far away? You may not get to talk with them often. This doesn't mean that you can't stay in touch, though. You can still "talk" to your friends by writing letters.

In friendly letters, you can share ideas and tell about things you are interested in. You can ask your friends about their activities. Your friends can write to you to let you know what they are doing.

You write letters for other reasons, too. You write to invite someone to a special event or to say thank you. In this chapter, you will learn to write friendly letters, invitations, and thank-you notes.

# 1 Writing a Friendly Letter

> A **friendly letter** has five parts: the heading, the greeting, the body, the closing, and the signature.

You write friendly letters whenever you want to share news with a friend. Look at the sample letter on page 245. Then read about the five parts.

## 1. Heading

The heading tells where you are when you write the letter. Your house number and street name are on the first line. The city, state, and ZIP codes are on the second line. The date is on the third line.

Look at the heading on the sample letter. Notice where the heading is placed. The lines of the heading begin near the middle of the paper. All three begin at the same place.

## 2. Greeting

The greeting is the way you say "hello" in a letter. Here are some different greetings you could use.

*Dear Ann,    Hi, Ann,    Hello, Ann,*

Read the greeting in the sample letter. See where it is placed. It is on a line by itself. Skip a line between the heading and the greeting. The greeting begins with a capital letter and ends with a comma. It is placed near the left edge of the paper.

**Sample Friendly Letter**

**Heading**
1748 Wharton Drive
Cleveland, Ohio 44101
March 14, 1988

**Greeting**
Dear Bill,

**Body**
I still have my stamp collection. Now it is almost as big as your collection. Yesterday I went to the post office and bought some new wildlife stamps. Three stamps have water birds on them and two have forest animals. Maybe we could trade stamps through the mail. If you like, I'll send you a list of my stamps.

**Closing**
Your friend,

**Signature**
Sam

### 3. Body

The body of the letter is your message. Write about things your friend will be interested in. Show interest in what your friend is doing, too. Look at the letter that Sam wrote to Bill. Sam told Bill about his hobby. He offered to trade stamps.

Indent the first line of the body. Write your ideas in sentences. Use correct punctuation.

### 4. Closing

The closing is the part of the letter when you say "goodbye." Here are some different closings.

*Your friend,   Sincerely,   Yours truly,*

Always begin your closing with a capital letter. If the closing has two words, do not use a capital letter in the second word. Use a comma after the closing.

Find the closing on the sample letter. Notice that it is lined up under the heading. Skip a line between the body and the closing.

### 5. Signature

The signature is your name. If you are writing to a close friend, your first name is probably enough. Find the signature on the sample letter. Notice that it begins at the same place as the closing.

## Exercises  Writing a Friendly Letter

**A.** Find a sample in *List 2* to match each part of a friendly letter. Write the five parts from *List 1.* Next to each, write the letter of the matching part.

List 1
1. heading
2. greeting
3. body
4. closing
5. signature

List 2
a. Today was exciting! A team from a TV station visited our school. They took pictures. My class was on the 6:00 news!
b. Valerie
c. Dear Jamie,
d. Your cousin,
e. 543 Oakton Avenue
   Ames, Iowa 50010
   April 1, 1987

**B.** Use the sample parts of a letter from Exercise A. Write the parts on your paper in the correct places for a letter.

**C.** Write a friendly letter to a friend or a relative. Use your own address in the heading. You may tell about a real thing that has happened or an imaginary happening. Remember to write all five parts of a friendly letter.

247

# 2 Addressing an Envelope

> Every **envelope** needs an address, a return address, and a postage stamp.

Your letter must go into an envelope before you can send it. The envelope will protect your letter. Be sure your envelope has an address, a return address, and a postage stamp.

Look at the sample envelope below. Then read about the three things an envelope needs.

**Sample Envelope**

**Return address**

Carla Wilson
625 Kirby
Houston, Texas 77201

**Postage stamp**

**Your friend's name and address**

Miss Sarah Collins
4513 Grove Street
Detroit, Michigan 48112

## 1. The Address

Write three lines to tell where the letter should go.

*Line 1* Write the name of your friend. Be sure to use both the first name and the last name.

*Line 2* Write your friend's house number and the name or number of the street.

*Line 3* Write the city and the state your friend lives in. Then write the ZIP code number.

## 2. The Return Address

The return address is your own address. It is needed in case there is a problem with delivery. Perhaps your friend moved, or the address you wrote has a mistake in it. Then the post office may have to return the letter to you.

The return address has three lines, just like the address for your friend. Follow the same directions. Notice, however, where the return address is placed.

## 3. The Postage Stamp

Place the postage stamp in the upper right-hand corner of your envelope. If your letter is very heavy, it may need more stamps. Go to a post office if you are not sure. A postal worker will weigh your letter and tell you the right amount of postage.

**Exercise** **Addressing an Envelope**

Copy this envelope on your paper. Make it as big as a real envelope. Fill in the boxes. Write a friend's name and address in the correct place. Write your own address as the return address. Draw a stamp.

# 3 Writing an Invitation

> An **invitation** is a written note that you give or send. Invitations can be for a party or special event.

In an **invitation,** you invite someone to a special event. The event may be a birthday party at your home or a program at school. Your invitation must be clear and exact. It must give the following information.

1. **What** is the event? If it is a party, be sure to tell what kind of party.
2. **When** is the event? Tell the day and time.
3. **Where** is the event? Tell the address.

If you send your invitation, be sure you have the correct address. Write your envelope carefully. Send the invitation in time for people to answer you.

When you receive an invitation, it is important to answer it. Your answer should tell whether you are coming. If you cannot come, it is polite to give a reason. Use the same form as an invitation.

Here is an invitation to a birthday party. In an invitation, the heading may include only the date.

**Sample Invitation**

> February 20, 1988
>
> Dear Maria,
>     Please come to my eighth birthday party. It will be from noon to two o'clock on Saturday, March 5. We will be having a cookout. The party will be at my house, 478 Beechwood. I hope you can be there and join the fun.
>                     Your friend,
>                     Susie Cheng

Labels on the invitation: **What** (birthday party), **When** (noon to two o'clock on Saturday, March 5), **Where** (my house, 478 Beechwood).

## Exercises    Writing Invitations

**A.** Imagine that you are having a party at your home. Write an invitation for your party. Include all five parts of a letter. For your greeting, use *Dear Classmate*. Give all the needed information.

**B.** Exchange the invitation you wrote for Exercise A with a classmate. First, write a "yes" answer to your classmate's invitation. Second, write a "no" answer. Give a reason.

# 4 Writing a Thank-You Note

> A **thank-you note** shows that you like what someone did for you.

You like someone to thank you when you do something nice. Other people feel the same way. Here are some times you may want to write a thank-you note.

1. You receive a gift.
2. Someone does a special favor for you.
3. You stay at a friend's house overnight.

In your thank-you note, say exactly what you are thankful for. Also, say something nice about the gift or favor. Send your note soon after you receive the gift or favor. If you wait too long, you may forget.

A thank-you note has all five parts of a letter: heading, greeting, body, closing, and signature. Find the five parts in the following note.

**Sample Thank-You Note**

> September 5, 1987
>
> Dear Aunt Meg and Uncle Steve,
>
> I've been telling all my friends about my visit to your farm. I miss hearing the rooster crow in the morning. My alarm clock doesn't sound as friendly. Thank you for inviting me. I had lots of fun.
>
> Your nephew,
> Cliff

**Exercises**    **Writing Thank-You Notes**

**A.** You stayed at your friend's house. Your friend's parents took you both to an art fair. Then you all went out for ice cream. Write a thank-you note.

**B.** Imagine that you received a talking robot for your birthday. Write a thank-you note for the gift.

# Using English in Cursive Writing

When you write letters, you present yourself to people. Your handwriting does this for you. Let them know you care enough to use your best handwriting. Whoever gets your letter will want to read every word.

It is disappointing to receive a letter that is hard to read. When you write, form each letter carefully. If you do not, your words may look misspelled. Look at this example. The cursive *d* can look like *cl* when it is poorly formed.

*clown     down     clown*

Follow these guides when you write in cursive.
1. Write on the baseline.
2. Keep your capital letters a full space tall.
3. Most lowercase letters are a half-space tall. However, some go above the midline.

## Exercise   Writing a Letter in Cursive

Use lined paper. Write a letter to someone who lives in another part of the United States. Explain that your class is interested in knowing what it's like to live in other parts of the country. Ask questions about school, sports, and weather.

Use your best cursive writing. Be sure to include the five parts of a friendly letter. Then address an envelope.

# Chapter 16 Review

**A. Writing a Friendly Letter** Here are the mixed-up parts of a letter. Write them in the correct order. Sign your own name.

Your pal,

Dear Dale,

>136 Green Briar Road
>Pueblo, Colorado 81001
>October 10, 1987

>   I really miss you since you moved away. How do you like your new school? Have you met friends in your neighborhood? Maybe we will get to see each other over summer vacation.

**B. Addressing an Envelope** On your paper, draw a rectangle as big as a real envelope. Address the envelope to Dale Carter, 1114 Pontiac, Newport, Maine 04953. Write your own address as the return address. Draw a stamp.

**C. Writing a Thank-You Note** Pretend you really have a friend name Dale, whom you wrote to in Exercise A. You have spent one week of summer vacation at Dale's house. You went to a swimming pool, a picnic, and the movies. Write a thank-you note to Dale. Tell how nice your visit was.

# Chapter 17

# Thinking Clearly

"Everybody loves Krispy Peanuts! Buy some today! You'll love Krispy Peanuts, too!"

Have you ever read or heard advertising like this? Do you always believe what advertisers say? Do you ever think about what they are saying?

Advertising is not the only thing you should think carefully about. You are always reading and hearing new ideas. You must think about each idea carefully. Then you can decide which ideas you want to believe.

In this chapter, you will learn about good thinking skills. You will learn to tell whether statements are fair or unfair. You will also find out how to explain your opinion to others.

# 1 Facts and Opinions

> **Facts** are true statements. They can be proved.
> **Opinions** are a person's feelings about something.

Facts are true statements that can be proved. Here is an example of a fact.

The temperature is zero degrees.

Opinions are a person's feelings about something. Look at these opinions.

"It's too cold out."
"I love cold weather."

People can have different opinions about the same thing. Some people dislike cold weather. Other people like it because they can ski or ice skate. Those people may say that the temperature of zero is just right.

Can you tell which of these statements are facts and which are opinions?

1. Orange is a pretty color.
2. The colors yellow and red make orange.
3. Jack o'lanterns are scary.
4. Jack o'lanterns are pumpkins with carved faces.

You hear and read many ideas. Make sure that you don't settle for someone else's opinion. Look for facts instead. Then you can form your own opinion.

**Exercises** **Seeing the Difference Between Facts and Opinions**

**A.** Here is a list of statements. Some are facts and some are opinions. Number your paper from 1 to 10. Write **F** for facts and **O** for opinions.

1. Fall is the nicest time of year.
2. Many trees lose their leaves in the fall.
3. It would be fun to be a bird.
4. Birds can fly.
5. Clouds hold water.
6. Clouds are beautiful.
7. Potatoes grow underground.
8. Potatoes taste delicious!
9. Bees have stingers.
10. Bees are dangerous.

**B.** Read the following facts. Then write one opinion about each fact.

Example: Blue and yellow mixed together make green. (fact)
Blue cars are nicer than red cars. (opinion)

1. This sweater is made of wool.
2. *Goggles* is the name of a book.
3. The Science Fair is next Tuesday.
4. Our swim team won a trophy.
5. We get milk from cows.

# Forming an Opinion

> An opinion should be backed up with facts.

Do you like pizza? Do you dislike long car rides? Do you think children should learn to swim?

When you answer these questions, you are giving your opinions. People may have different opinions about the same thing. That is why it is important to be able to explain your opinion.

## Presenting Your Opinion

When you have an opinion, state it clearly. Back it up with facts. Here is an example.

Carla's class was choosing a science project. Carla wanted the class to start an ant farm. She read about how ants live and what they eat. Then she gave her opinion. Here is the way Carla presented her opinion.

> Our class should make an ant farm. Watching the ants would teach us about another form of life. We could learn how they work and live. We could watch them dig tunnels and care for their eggs. We could feed the ants pieces of lettuce and bread crumbs.

## Making Decisions

Sometimes people do not support their opinions. It is up to you to find out more information. Think about this situation.

Suppose you want to get a pet. Your brother says a raccoon would be a good pet. Your sister says a raccoon would be a terrible pet. Which person is right? Should you try to get a raccoon?

First, you must decide whether your brother and sister are giving facts or opinions. In this case, it is easy to decide. You can see that both people are telling their feelings. They are giving opinions. Now you must find the facts.

## Finding Facts

A fact is true. It can be proved. Before you form an opinion, find facts about the subject. Here are some ways you could find facts about raccoons.

1. **You can look at books.** For example, suppose you want to know what raccoons eat. You could find out by looking in the encyclopedia under *Raccoons*.
2. **You can talk with people.** Perhaps you can talk to a pet store owner, a zoo keeper, or a forest ranger. You can ask about the habits of raccoons.

When you know some facts, you can decide for yourself whether a raccoon is a good pet. You can separate fact from opinion. You think about the subject clearly. You form your own opinion and make a decision.

## Exercises     Explaining Your Opinion

**A.** Choose one of these opinions. Do you agree or disagree with it? Tell two facts to back up your opinion.

1. Homework should not be given on weekends.
2. We should grow our own vegetables.
3. We should help to clean our neighborhood.

**B.** Read about the decisions that Jay and Cindy must make. Then answer the question below each paragraph.

1. Jay lives out in the country. He has a cat named Tippy. Tippy loves to roam outside. Jay and his family will soon move to the city. His parents say Tippy will not enjoy the city. Jay thinks Tippy will be fine.

How can Jay find some facts to back up his opinion?

2. Cindy's club needs to earn money for a trip. The club can sell greeting cards or have a bake sale. The club members must choose one of those ways to earn money.

What questions should the club members ask before they make a choice?

# 3 Generalizations

> A **generalization** is a general statement about a whole group of objects or actions. A generalization can be fair or unfair.

In part 1, you learned that you should separate facts from opinions. Sometimes this is not easy. Opinions often sound like facts. By mistake, you may use these opinions to make a decision. Then your decision might not be a good one.

One kind of opinion that may trick you is a generalization. A **generalization** is a statement about a whole group of things. A generalization may be fair or unfair.

Here is an example of a generalization.

All snakes are dangerous.

This generalization seems to be based on facts. Perhaps the speaker knows some facts about dangerous snakes. However, it is unfair to say that all snakes are dangerous. Here is a better way to make this statement.

Some snakes are dangerous.

263

Words like *some, most, usually,* and *seldom* can often turn a generalization into a true statement. Here is another example.

Snacks are not good for you.

Can that be true? Can all snacks be bad for you? A fact may be that snacks often ruin your appetite for meals. But *often* does not mean *always.* Here are better ways to say this.

Some snacks are not good for you.
Snacks sometimes ruin your appetite.

### Listening to Commercials

People may use generalizations to persuade you to do something. Ads on television or in magazines often use generalizations. Here is an example.

Everybody loves Champo games.

Can *everybody* know about Champo games? How can *everybody* love them? When you read or hear a generalization like that, try to change it into a fact. Here is a statement that may be a fact.

Some people like Champo games.

Now it is up to you to decide whether you agree.
Listen to commercials and read ads carefully. Use clear thinking to decide whether to buy things. Look for generalizations. Try to change them into statements that may be true. Then you can better decide whether to buy these things.

**Exercises**    **Understanding Generalizations**

**A.** Read each of these generalizations. Write **Fair** or **Unfair** on your paper to tell what kind each one is.

1. Everybody likes spinach.
2. Some people like spinach.
3. Thick books are harder to read than thin books.
4. All animals need food.
5. Sunny days are warmer than cloudy days.
6. Some children like cereal for breakfast.
7. Tall people are good at sports.
8. Good swimmers are not afraid of water.
9. It's always dark at 6:00 p.m.
10. All children love Snappo Cereal!

**B.** Listen to several radio or television commercials. Read some newspaper or magazine ads.

Find two generalizations that the advertisers make about their products. Write the generalizations. If you can, change each generalization into a statement that may be true. Write your new statements.

# Using English in Math

You can often use math facts to help you make a decision or back up your opinion. Read these opinions and facts.

**Opinion:** I don't think the desk will fit in my room.
   **Fact:** The desk is four feet wide. The space is three feet wide.
**Opinion:** It's too cold to go swimming.
   **Fact:** The temperature outside is 40 degrees.

Many math facts can be proved by using measuring instruments. For instance, a doctor uses a thermometer and scale to find out facts about your health. Measuring instruments you may have used are a ruler, yardstick, and clock. What facts can those instruments give you?

## Exercise  Using Math Facts To Make a Decision

Read the following questions. Tell which math instrument you can use to help you make a decision. Write a possible decision using a math fact.

1. Should I wear a light or a heavy jacket?
2. Do I need more postage to mail this package?
3. Will I have enough flour to bake the bread?
4. Is this shade the right size for my window?
5. Will I have enough time to get to the library?

# Chapter 17 Review

**A. Finding Facts and Opinions** Number your paper from 1 to 5. For each statement, write **F** for fact or **O** for opinion. Then try to write a fact for each opinion.

1. Apples grow on trees.
2. Tan is the nicest shade of brown.
3. Bears hibernate in the winter.
4. Pippi Longstocking is the smartest character in that book.
5. George Washington was the best president of the United States.

**B. Thinking Clearly** A word is missing in each sentence. Write the sentences. Use these words to fill in the blanks.

    facts    decision    clearly

1. State your opinion _____.
2. Use _____ to back up your opinion.
3. When you make a _____, it is important to know the facts.

**C. Identifying Generalizations** Read the following generalizations. Number your paper from 1 to 5. Write **Fair** or **Unfair** for each generalization.

1. Cats and dogs don't like each other.
2. Arizona is sometimes hot.
3. Some basketball players are tall.
4. Everybody loves pizza.
5. April is always rainy.

# Chapter 18

# Getting To Know the Library

Where can you find dinosaurs, spaceships, and presidents all in the same place? Where can you travel to the North Pole and to Africa without leaving the room? All of these things can happen in one place—the library.

The library is a good place to find a book about anything that interests you. In this chapter, you will discover how the card catalog helps you find books. You will learn how to choose a book by looking at its parts. You will also learn to use an encyclopedia.

When you get to know the library, you will be able to choose books that will give you pleasure. The library will become one of your best friends.

# 1 Kinds of Books

> **Fiction books** tell about make-believe people and events. **Nonfiction books** tell facts and information. **Reference books** are a special kind of nonfiction book.

When you visit a library, you may be looking for a certain kind of book. You may want to read a story, or you may need to look for information.

A **fiction book** tells a story that someone has made up. The people and events are make-believe.

A **nonfiction book** tells about real people or events. Nonfiction books give facts and information. Look at these book titles. Can you tell which is nonfiction?

*The Three Wishes*    *All About Whales*

A **reference book** is a special kind of nonfiction book. Two kinds of reference books are the dictionary and the encyclopedia. You have already learned about the dictionary in Chapter 3. You will learn about the encyclopedia later in this chapter.

**Library books are arranged in a special way.** The fiction books are together in one section. They are in alphabetical order, by the author's last name. A book by E. B. White would come before a book by Laura Ingalls Wilder.

Nonfiction books are arranged by their subject. For example, all books about plants are put together. Reference books are grouped in a separate section.

## Exercises  Kinds of Books

**A.** Number your paper from 1 to 10. Look at the list of books below. Write **F** for fiction and **NF** for nonfiction books.

1. *Little Brown Bear*
2. *Metric Puzzles*
3. *Pueblo Indians*
4. *Encyclopedia of Art*
5. *Freaky Friday*
6. *Alice in Wonderland*
7. *How to Draw Cartoons*
8. *New World Dictionary*
9. *Madeline's Rescue*
10. *The Stars and Planets*

**B.** Fiction books are arranged in alphabetical order by the author's last name. Write these fiction titles in the correct order that you would find them in the library.

1. *Pippi Goes on Board* by Astrid Lindgren
2. *Betsy-Tacy* by Maud Hart Lovelace
3. *Prairie School* by Lois Lenski
4. *Mr. Twigg's Mistake* by Robert Lawson
5. *A Color of His Own* by Leo Lionni

**C.** You need a library card to take books out of the public library. Ask your librarian to help you get a library card. Many libraries ask you to fill out a form. Here is a sample form. Copy it on your paper. Fill in the information. Remember to print clearly.

```
┌─────────────────────────────────────────────┐
│        Library Card Application Form        │
│                                             │
│  Name _____ │
│  Address _____ │
│  Telephone Number _____ │
│  Parent's Name _____ │
│  Name of School _____ │
└─────────────────────────────────────────────┘
```

## 2 Using the Card Catalog

> The **card catalog** has title cards, author cards, and subject cards for books in the library.

The **card catalog** has cards that list every book in the library. The cards are in alphabetical order. They have information to help you find books.

You know that fiction and nonfiction books are kept in separate places. It is easy to find a fiction book if you know the author's name. If you know only the title, however, look for the **title card.** It will tell you the author's name so you can find the book.

What if you want to read books by one author but do not know the titles? The **author cards** will give you the information. Look for the author's last name.

How would you find a book about lions? You may not know the title of the book or the author's name. The **subject cards** for *Lions* will tell about lion books.

Look at these sample cards.

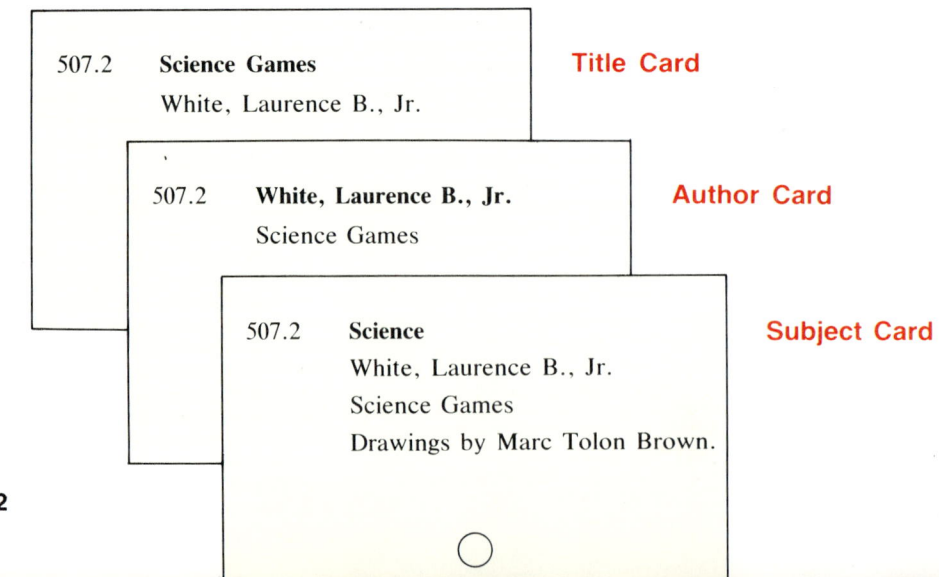

## Exercises  Using the Card Catalog

**A.** Write the kind of card you would use to find each book listed below. Write **author card, title card,** or **subject card.**

1. A book to tell you more about otters
2. A new book by Beverly Cleary
3. A book called *The Mystery of the Lost Keys* suggested by your friend
4. A book about pilgrims, for your Thanksgiving program
5. A book of poetry by Shel Silverstein

**B.** Look at this map of a library. Find where the card catalog is located. What else is shown on the map?

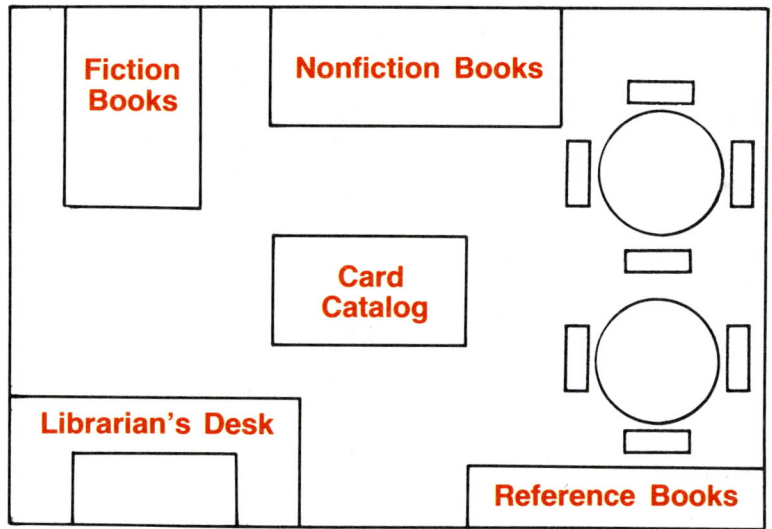

**C.** Visit your school library or your neighborhood library. Look to see where the fiction, nonfiction, and reference books are kept. Find the card catalog. Draw a map of that section of the library. If you wish, work with a partner.

# 3 The Parts of a Book

> The **title page** of a book tells the title and the author's name. The **table of contents** lists the names of the chapters in a book. The **index** is an alphabetical list of the subjects in a book.

When you look at the cover of a book, you see the title and the author's name. However, the cover may not tell you whether the book is one you want to read. If you look through the pages, you will have a better idea of what the book is about.

Every book has a **title page** at the beginning of the book. The title page gives the name of the book and the name of the person or people who wrote the book.

The **table of contents** comes right after the title page. The table of contents lists the chapters of the book. Page numbers tell where chapters begin. In nonfiction books, the names of the chapters can help you decide if the book tells about the subjects you need.

An **index** can be found in the back of most nonfiction books. The index is an alphabetical listing of the subjects or topics in the books. The index gives the page numbers where you can find information about the subjects.

```
INDEX
Accident(s), 136
    helping after, 151-153
    preventing, 146
Advertisements, 205
Air pollution, 185, 186
Alcohol, 170
    health problems caused by,
        170-171
Allergist, 127
Allergy, 126
American Dental Association, 78
Angry feelings, 11, 12, 22-24, 26
Asthma, 124
Audiologist, 54

Bacteria, 115
Basic food groups, 90
    kinds of, 90-95
Bicycle checkup, 140
```

## Exercises  Using the Parts of a Book

**A.** Look at the sample title page, table of contents, and index on pages 274 and 275. Write these sentences on your paper. Complete each one with the correct information.

1. The title of the book is _____.
2. The name of Chapter 1 is _____.
3. Page 22 is about _____.
4. Information on allergy can be found on page ___.
5. There are ___ pages about air pollution.

**B.** Imagine that you have written a nonfiction book. Think of a title for your book. Make a title page for it. Be sure your name is the author on the title page.

Now write a table of contents for your book. List the names of the first three chapters. Tell what page each chapter begins on.

Exchange papers with a friend. Tell your friend about your book. Ask your friend about his or her book.

# 4 Using an Encyclopedia

> **Encyclopedias** are reference books that give information about many subjects.

Often you go to the library to find information about a certain subject. If you go to the section with reference books, you will find **encyclopedias.** Usually, the encyclopedias are kept on a separate shelf.

The books in a set of encyclopedias are called **volumes.** On the side of each volume are a number and one or more letters. Subjects that begin with those letters are in that volume.

The volumes are in alphabetical order. To look up a subject, use the key word. For example, look up Birds of North America under *Bird* in the **B** volume. If the subject is a person, use the first letter of the last name. For example, information about Hans Christian Andersen would be in the **A** volume.

**BIRD**

**Birds of North America**

There are hundreds of species of birds in North America. The birds live in different kinds of habitats. Some birds live in grasslands and some near water. They live in cities, in forests, or in deserts.

### Exercises  Using an Encyclopedia

**A.** Look at Volume 9 in the set of encyclopedias below. Read this list of subjects. Write the subjects from the list that would be in that volume. Look for the key word.

1. Jane Addams
2. Jefferson Memorial
3. New Jersey
4. kangaroos
5. Lyndon B. Johnson
6. Kenya
7. cities of Japan
8. Francis Scott Key
9. kinds of trees
10. Johnny Appleseed

**B.** Look at the set of encyclopedias in the picture above. Tell which volume you will need for each subject in this list.

1. cactus plants
2. how money is made
3. weather in Hawaii
4. Albert Einstein
5. starting an aquarium
6. where opossums live
7. Gwendolyn Brooks
8. North Dakota
9. early locomotives
10. the White House

# Using English in Social Studies

A special kind of nonfiction book tells about the life of a real person. It is called a **biography.**

The biographies of people from the history of our country are in your library. Some are about people who lived long ago. Others are about people doing things today. When we read a biography, we learn about a person's life. While we are learning, we are enjoying a fascinating, true story.

You can find biographies in a special section of the library. The biography books are in alphabetical order, by the person's last name.

## Exercise   Reading and Sharing a Biography

Find a biography to read. Here are some ideas of people to read about. Your teacher or librarian can suggest others. Choose a person you would like to know more about.

Helen Keller
John F. Kennedy
Clara Barton
George Rodgers Clark
Maria Tallchief
Martin Luther King, Jr.

Tell your friends about the person you read about. Here are some ideas for sharing a biography.

1. Write a paragraph about the person. Draw a picture about one event in the person's life.
2. Pretend you are the person in the book. Have classmates ask you questions about your life.

# Chapter 18 Review

**A. Kinds of Books** Read this list of books. Write **F** for fiction and **NF** for nonfiction. Add **R** for reference books.

1. *Beezus and Ramona*
2. *World Book Encyclopedia*
3. *Strawberry Girl*
4. *Sign Language*
5. *Mystery of the Magic Mountain*
6. *Globe Student Dictionary*
7. *Babar the Elephant*
8. *Abraham Lincoln*
9. *Blue Fairy Tales*
10. *How to Raise Goldfish and Guppies*

**B. The Card Catalog** Look at this drawer from a card catalog. Choose the books from the list of titles that would have cards in this drawer. Write the book titles.

1. *Tornado!*
2. *Theodore Roosevelt*
3. *Teddy's Birthday*
4. *The Pied Piper of Hamelin*
5. *Mother Goose* by Tasha Tudor

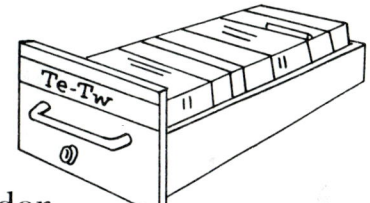

**C. Using the Parts of a Book** The book you are using has a title page, a table of contents, and an index. Write the answers to these questions about this book.

1. What is the title of this book?
2. What is the name of Chapter 3?
3. On what page does the poetry chapter begin?
4. Look in the index to find where synonyms are taught.
5. How many pages tell something about addressing envelopes? Look in the index.

# Chapter 19

# Writing a Report

A reporter gathers and gives information to others. You are sometimes a reporter, too. You gather information to write a science report about animals you are studying. You might write a social studies report about community helpers or Hopi Indian dolls. Sometimes you write book reports.

In this chapter, you will learn some ways to help you write better reports. You will use the writing process you have been studying. You will learn how to use that process for writing reports.

# 1 Thinking About Reports

> A **report** is a group of paragraphs that gives facts. The facts tell about a subject.

Often you will write a report about something you are studying. Suppose that you are studying ways people travel. You are asked to write a report about air travel. What might your report be like?

**Read and Think.** Gerald decided to write about an airport. He wrote three paragraphs for his report. As you read, notice how each paragraph tells about one part of the airport.

### An Airport

Airplane travel starts in an airport. Passengers go to buildings called terminals. The terminal is the place where travelers buy tickets. The terminal has places to sit and rest. It also has restaurants and shops.

Another important part of an airport is the control tower. Workers in the tower direct the planes in the air and on the ground. They tell pilots when to take off and when to land.

The largest part of the airport is used for runways. Airplanes take off and land on runways. White lines painted on them guide pilots during the day. At night, lights on the runways guide the pilots.

**Think and Discuss.** Gerald told many facts in his report. Read the report again. Talk about these questions with your class.

1. What parts of the airport did Gerald write about?
2. What is the first paragraph about?
3. Tell three facts that are in the first paragraph.
4. What is the main idea of the second paragraph?
5. What is one fact Gerald told about runways?
6. Why do you think Gerald wrote three paragraphs instead of one or two?

### Now It's Your Turn

You have read a report that gives information about a subject. The facts in the report are grouped into paragraphs. Now you will learn steps to write your own report.

## 2 Prewriting: Choosing a Subject and Taking Notes

> Plan a report before you write. Choose a subject and find facts about it. Take notes about the facts.

Every report needs a plan. Read about these prewriting steps before you write a report.

### Choosing a Subject

Many times your teacher gives you a subject for a report. Sometimes, though, you might choose your own subject. Where do you begin?

First, make a list of subjects that interest you. Maybe you like racing cars or photography. Next, list subjects you would like to find out more about. Perhaps you would like to learn about a police station or a greenhouse. List as many subjects as you can.

Go over your list. Choose two or three subjects that you like best. Decide which of these subjects would make a good report. Ask these questions.

1. Which subject do I like best?
2. Can I tell about it in two or three paragraphs?
3. Can I find out enough information about my subject?

When you have chosen your subject, you are ready to gather information about it.

## Taking Notes

The next step is taking notes. Notes are short ways of writing facts about your subject. Notes do not have to be sentences.

To gather facts, you can read about your subject in books. You can ask people who know about your subject. You can write the facts you know already.

Sheila decided to write about firefighters. She read some books about firefighters. She even visited a firehouse. Here are her notes.

*pumper with hose*
*eat in kitchen*
*save property*
*ladder trucks*
*sleep in big room*
*rescue people*
*dog with black spots*
*spray water*
*rescue trucks*

**Exercise** **Choosing A Subject and Taking Notes**

Choose a subject for your report. If you need more ideas, look at the list called Topics for a Report on page 335 of the **Power Handbook**.

Find facts about your subject. Write the facts as notes. Use reference books in the library.

# 3 Making a Plan and Writing a Draft

> Make a writing plan from your notes. Write a draft from your plan.

You have written facts about a subject. Now you must put the facts in order. Some tell about the same main idea. You can put them together in an outline.

## Making an Outline

An outline is a writing plan. It groups main ideas and the facts that go with them. The main ideas are labeled with a Roman numeral. The facts follow.

Sheila read and thought about her notes. She saw that her facts were about three main ideas. Look at the outline she made for her writing plan.

Firefighters

I. What firefighters do
spray water
rescue people
save property

II. Fire trucks
pumper with hose
ladder trucks
rescue trucks

III. Life in firehouse
sleep in big room
eat in kitchen

Notice that Sheila left out her note about the dog. It did not fit any of her main ideas.

Read your notes and put them in outline form. Write each main idea after a Roman numeral. Write the facts that go with that idea under it.

## Writing a Draft

Your outline will help you write a draft. Each main idea will become the topic sentence of a paragraph. The facts under that main idea will become the other sentences in the paragraph.

Start with your first main idea. Write a topic sentence that states the idea. Then write the facts as sentences in the paragraph. Start your second paragraph with your second main idea. Continue writing, using all your main ideas and facts.

## Exercises   Making a Plan and Writing a Draft

**A. Making an Outline** Read these notes about a farm. Think of three main ideas they tell about. Write an outline from the notes. Group the notes under three main ideas.

soybeans   chickens   pigs   tractor
plow       corn       wheat  horses

**B. Writing Your Draft** Use your notes to make an outline for your report. Then write a draft from your outline.

# 4 Revising and Sharing a Report

> Revise your draft to make it better. Proofread it and make a final copy for sharing.

## Revising Your Report

Read your draft carefully. Can you make it better? You may want to add or take out some ideas. Now is the time to revise your report.

Ask yourself the questions listed below. Mark the changes on your paper.

---

**Guides for Revising a Report**

1. Is the report interesting?
2. Is the report easy to understand? Are the paragraphs in an order that makes sense?
3. Does each sentence tell about the main idea? Should any sentence be added or taken away?

---

Read the last paragraph of Sheila's report. She found some mistakes and marked several changes.

*(Add describing words.)*

*(I need an ending sentence.)*

Firefighters sleep and eat in the firehouse. They sleep upstairs ^*in a big room*. They cook their meals in a ^*tiny* kitchen. Firefighters stay in the firehouse, ^*and* ~~They~~ wait for the bell to ring. *They are always ready to fight a fire.*

*(Make into one sentence.)*

## Finishing Your Report

You are ready to proofread your report. Look for any mistakes in capital letters, punctuation, and spelling. Then, write your final copy neatly. Make all the changes you have marked.

Read Sheila's finished report.

---

Firefighters

Firefighters have an exciting job. They rush to a fire. They spray water to put the fire out. They rescue people and try to save property from burning.

Firefighters use three kinds of trucks. Pumper trucks have large hoses used for spraying water. Ladder trucks help firefighters go up high on tall ladders. Rescue trucks carry tools for special jobs.

Firefighters sleep and eat in the firehouse. They sleep upstairs in a big room. They cook their meals in a tiny kitchen. Firefighters stay in the firehouse and wait for the bell to ring. They are always ready to fight a fire.

---

### Exercises    Revising and Sharing a Report

**A. Revising and Finishing Your Report** Make changes to improve your report. Proofread it carefully, using the guides on page 332 in the **Power Handbook.** Make a neat final copy.

**B. Sharing Your Report** Plan an oral report to give to your class. Practice saying it aloud. Use your outline to help you.

# Speaking and Listening

## An Interview

You can interview someone to gather information for a report. An **interview** is a meeting with another person. At this meeting, you ask questions. The answers you get will give you information.

To have an interview, you must be prepared.

1. First, set up a time and place to meet the person.
2. Then, prepare a list of questions to ask.

When you meet with the person at the interview, ask your questions. As the person answers, listen carefully. Make notes about what the person says. Don't write every word. Write only the main ideas.

After your questions are finished, thank the person politely for giving you an interview.

### Exercise   Telling About a Career

Do you know someone who has an interesting job? Ask the person whether you may interview him or her. Follow the suggestions above. Find out all you can about that person's job. Here are some sample questions:

1. How did you prepare for your career?
2. What is the best part of your job?
3. Which people help you in your work?

After your interview, write your notes in outline form. Give an oral report. Tell about the career you discussed.

# Creative Writing

**A.** Dorothy found the Land of Oz. Alice walked through a mirror and ended up in Wonderland. Make up your own imaginary place. Write a short report about it. Describe your imaginary land and the people who live there. If anything unusual happens there, tell what it is.

**B.** A strange new animal is on display at the zoo. It combines parts of two different animals. It could have the neck of the giraffe and the body of a rabbit. It could be an ostrich with a turtle shell.

Write a short report about this animal. Tell what it looks like and how it moves. Give the animal a name.

**C.** Pretend that you are a famous reporter for the *Evening Star Newspaper*. Yesterday, someone in your city was given an award for bravery. Make up and write the facts about this important story. Tell *who*, *what*, *where*, *when*, and *why* in your report.

# Using English in Reading

You read some books for fun. You read other books to get information. Sometimes you want to tell someone about a book you read. Telling about books is one way of sharing them.

Another way to share books is to write a book report. A **book report** should answer these questions.

1. What is the title?
2. Who is the author?
3. What is the book about?
4. Why do you like the book?

You tell the title and author to let your readers know what book you are reporting on. You tell something about the book to get your readers interested. For example, you could tell one strange or exciting event that happens in the book. Don't tell the ending, however. Let the readers find out for themselves. Finally, tell why you liked the book.

**Exercise** Writing and Sharing a Book Report

Choose a book you like. Write a book report that will get the readers interested. Follow the four guides listed above. Draw a picture to go with your book report. Share it with your class.

# Chapter 19 Review

**A. Thinking About Reports** Read this paragraph from a report. Then answer the questions below.

> Many people come to live in the United States. Some people come to find new jobs. Some come to join friends or family. Most people come to have better lives.

1. What is the main idea of the paragraph?
2. How many sentences give reasons to tell why people come to the United States?

**B. Making an Outline** The notes below are for a report on honeybees. The notes fit under three main headings: **Kinds of bees, Parts of a bee,** and **What bees make.** Make an outline. Use outline form to write the main headings and the notes that go with each.

| stinger | queen | honey | legs |
| wax | feelers | eyes | workers |

**C. Using Proofreading Marks** Rewrite this paragraph from a report. Make the changes that are marked.

¶ Strawberries grow in rows. You find a row with big red ~~berrys~~ *berries*. Sometimes, you have to look for the hidden fruit *under the leaves*. then you start *picking berries and* filling your ~~B~~basket.

# Chapter 20

# Using Capital Letters

Sometimes we use signals to get someone's attention. The signal may be a wave, or a word, or a whistle. In writing, we also have signals. One signal is a capital letter. When a word starts with a capital letter, it tells us something about the word. It can signal that the word is a name or the beginning of a sentence. Capitals may signal other things, too.

In this chapter, you will learn about the ways to use capital letters. Understanding how capital letters are used will help you when you read. It will also help you write more clearly.

# 1 Names of People and Pets

> Begin names of persons or pets with **capital letters.** Capitalize initials, titles of people, and the word *I*.

Here are some rules for using capital letters.

**1. Capitalize the name of every person or pet.** Some names have more than one word. Use a capital letter at the beginning of every word.

    Mary      Robert
    Lassie    Robert Edward Lee

**2. Capitalize initials.** People often write only the first letter of a name. That first letter is called an **initial.** Use a period after the initial.

    Mary M. Bethune    Robert E. Lee

**3. Capitalize a title in a name.** A title is a special word that is used with a name. It is part of the name.

Here are some titles used often. After each title is the short form, or abbreviation. Notice that the abbreviation begins with a capital letter and ends with a period.

    Mister    Mr.    Doctor    Dr.
    Mistress  Mrs.   Junior   Jr.

**4. Capitalize the word *I*.** The word *I* is used in place of a name. It is always capitalized.

**Exercises** Using Capital Letters for Names of People, Pets, and *I*

**A.** Write these names. Use capital letters where they are needed.

1. pearl s. buck
2. mr. evans
3. susan b. anthony
4. dr. mitchell
5. conchita
6. martin luther king, jr.
7. miss stern
8. charlie brown
9. mrs. morrow
10. thomas a. edison

**B.** Write these sentences. Use capital letters correctly.

1. I wish i could skate like tiffany chin.
2. Tomiko and sonya like to trade cards.
3. May i work on your computer?
4. The band plays marches by john philip sousa.
5. We helped mr. antoni train his sheep dog.
6. The pitcher threw the ball to marcy.
7. Lois saw doug henning do a magic show.
8. Eli opened the door for mrs. kaplan.
9. Did dr. olson listen to your heart?
10. I think harriet tubman was a brave person.

# 2 Particular Places and Things

> Capitalize every important word in the name of a special place or thing.

Names of particular places and things are special. Like names of people and pets, they are capitalized.

    Ames, Iowa    Liberty Bell    Hall of Fame

Many of these names have more than one word. Capitalize every important word in the name. Do not capitalize little words such as *a, the,* or *of*.

**1. Capitalize names of days, months, and holidays.** Also, capitalize abbreviations for days and months.

    Monday    Tues.
    June        Oct.
    Thanksgiving
    Fourth of July

**2. Capitalize the names of special buildings.**

    the White House    Union School

**3. Capitalize names of streets and roads.** Also, capitalize abbreviations of streets and roads.

    Lake Avenue    Lake Ave.
    South Fourth Street    So. Fourth St.
    Randolph Road    Randolph Rd.

4. Capitalize names of towns, cities, states, and countries.

    Carbondale, Illinois    Italy

Some names for groups of people are made from the names of places. Capitalize those names.

    Canada—Canadians    Hawaii—Hawaiians

## Exercises  Using Capital Letters for Names of Particular Places and Things

**A.** Write these names of places and things. Use capital letters where they are needed.

1. midpark school
2. united kingdom
3. maple street
4. florida
5. gulf of mexico
6. sunday
7. memorial day
8. ohio
9. february
10. ridge road

**B.** Write these sentences. Use capital letters correctly.

1. My lucky day is friday.
2. Laura camped near flagstaff, arizona.
3. Mario saw a deer cross willow road.
4. The carnival is coming on july 15.
5. There are pyramids in egypt.
6. Is sixth street closed for the rally?
7. We are going to a picnic on labor day.
8. The empire state building is in new york.
9. Marconi was an italian inventor.
10. The halloween parade is at madison school.

# 3 First Words

> First words are capitalized in sentences, quotations, poems, parts of letters, and outlines.

**1. Capitalize the first word of every sentence.**

| | |
|---|---|
| This program is funny. | Statement |
| Do you watch it often? | Question |
| Please turn up the sound. | Command |
| How silly the story is! | Exclamation |

**2. Capitalize the first word of a quotation.** A quotation means the exact words a person says. Quotation marks (" ") show the beginning and ending of a quotation.

Louisa asked, "May I help?"
"Yes, thank you," said Fred.

**3. In most poems, capitalize the first word in every line.**

One day a funny kind of man
Came walking down the street.
He wore a shoe upon his head,
And hats upon his feet.
—NATALIE JOAN, "A Funny Man"

**4. Capitalize the first word in the greeting and in the closing of a letter.**

Dear Jean,     Sincerely,     Yours truly,

**5. Capitalize the first word of each idea in an outline.** An outline is a list of important ideas about a subject.

> Animals of the Far North
>   I. Huskies
>   II. Polar bears
>   III. Walrus

## Exercise   Using Capital Letters for First Words

Write the following sentences, poem, letter, and outline. Use capital letters where they are needed.

1. the magician made the bird disappear.
2. angela said, "the slide is slippery."
3. do penguins know how to fly?
4. "grab the leash!" yelled kelly.

5. behold the duck.
   it does not cluck.
   a cluck it lacks.
   it quacks.   —OGDEN NASH, "The Duck"

6. dear juan,
      i hope you can visit us this summer. dad says he will take us camping. there is also a new bike trail. please ask your parents.
                     your friend,
                     ricci

7. Life on a Desert
     I. animals
     II. plants
     III. people

# 4 Titles

> Capitalize the first, last, and every other important word in a title.

Capitalize most of the words in titles of books, movies, television programs, or other long writings. Always capitalize the first and last words and every important word. Do not capitalize little words like *and, of, in,* and *the* unless they come first.

| | |
|---|---|
| **Book** | *Where the Wild Things Are* |
| **Movie** | *Return of the Jedi* |
| **TV Program** | *Little House on the Prairie* |

Notice the kind of print in the samples above. This is called **italic** print. It is used in books to show titles. When you write the title of a book, underline the complete title.

*Where the Wild Things Are*

Do not underline titles of short works like stories, poems, or reports. Use quotation marks instead.

| | |
|---|---|
| **Story** | "The Wind and the Sun" |
| **Poem** | "Speaking of Cows" |
| **Report** | "How To Raise Goldfish" |

## Exercises  Using Capital Letters in Titles

**A.** Write these titles. Use capital letters where they are needed. Copy the quotation marks and underlining shown.

1. pets in a jar
2. "flowers of the forest"
3. walter the lazy mouse
4. "teach your dog tricks"
5. pippi longstocking
6. "the swing"
7. "little snail"
8. the bear scouts
9. space cat
10. the wizard of oz

**B.** Write these sentences. Use capital letters correctly. Underline the titles in italic print.

1. my dog looks like sandy in *annie.*
2. the boy is brave in *my father's dragon.*
3. "henry reed's journey" is a funny story.
4. *ribsy* is about a dog that gets into trouble.
5. *the cat in the hat* made celia laugh.
6. "my shadow" is a clever poem.
7. "the fox and the crow" is a fable.
8. leslie knows the poem "casey at the bat."
9. *oliver* is a movie about a boy in england.
10. i used to watch *the electric company.*

**C. Writing** Write a paragraph about your favorite movie or television program. Give the title and tell what you like about the movie or program. Share your paragraph with a friend.

# Exercises for Mastery  Chapter 20
## Using Capital Letters

**A. Using Capital Letters for Names of People, Pets, and I** Write these sentences. Use capital letters where they are needed.

1. The first man on the moon was neil armstrong.
2. This story is about a horse named flicka.
3. May heidi and i swim in the pool?
4. My favorite writer is dr. seuss.
5. We are planning a birthday surprise for ms. newman.
6. Start to run when mr. reid blows the whistle.
7. We won the game when i hit a home run in the ninth inning.
8. My kitten is called fluffy.
9. The puppy rolled over for rosa.
10. A. a. milne wrote about a bear named winnie-the-pooh.

**B. Using Capital Letters for Names of Particular Places and Things** Write these names of places and things. Use capital letters where they are needed.

1. oxford school
2. grand canyon
3. park avenue
4. mojave desert
5. ohio river
6. france
7. tuesday
8. april
9. main st.
10. south america

**C. Using Capital Letters for First Words** Write the sentences, poem, letter, and outline. Use capital letters where they are needed.

1. do not feed the bears.
2. the guard said, "the bridge is going up."
3. how tall is the washington monument?
4. is a caterpillar ticklish?
   well, it's always my belief
   that he giggles, as he wiggles
   across a hairy leaf.
   —MONICA SHANNON, "Only My Opinion"
5. dear adriana,
     you left your swimsuit here. i will mail it to you. please write.
               sincerely,
               kirsten
6. uses of plants
     I. food and clothing
    II. medicine
   III. decoration and pleasure

**D. Using Capital Letters in Titles** Write the titles, using capital letters. Copy the quotation marks and underlining.

1. <u>harry, the dirty dog</u>
2. "three rolls and a pretzel"
3. "magic tricks you can learn"
4. <u>the giants' farm</u>
5. "the elephant's child"

# Using Grammar in Writing

**A.** Dumbo is an elephant that flies. Lassie is a dog that has exciting adventures. Write a story or a poem about an unusual animal. Name the animal. Tell what it can do. Tell about one or two people the animal knows or meets.

**B.** Would you like to tell something to a character in a story you have read? Perhaps you thought of a way the character could have avoided some trouble. Write a letter to the character. Pretend the character is your friend. Tell the character about your ideas. Name the book or story. You might tell the character how you liked the story.

**C. Using Capital Letters in Social Studies** A map has four directions. They are **north, south, east,** and **west.** Find your state on a map. Write the name of your state and the capital city. Tell what state, ocean, or country lies in each direction from where you live. Use capital letters for the places you name.

# Chapter 20 Review

**A. Using Capital Letters in Names** Write these sentences. Use capital letters correctly.

1. i saw a dinosaur egg at the abbott museum.
2. four President's heads are carved on mt. rushmore.
3. dr. elizabeth blackwell opened a hospital in new york city.
4. mr. allen's pet is an australian dog.
5. valentine's day is february 14.
6. davy crockett grew up in tennessee.
7. ms. arnez let sam use the stopwatch.
8. our class read about martha washington.
9. val rode in a carriage on fifth avenue.
10. mark twain's real name was samuel l. clemens.

**B. Using Capitals Correctly** Write these sentences. Use capital letters where they are needed.

1. "did you watch the world series?" fred asked.
2. kermit treats miss piggy very well.
3. what a big jaw that shark has!
4. a space center is in cape canaveral, florida.
5. "that snake is not dangerous," mrs. tyler said.
6. jane addams helped new americans.
7. "elephants' tusks are teeth," lena said.
8. connie said, "the track is too wet to race."
9. walt disney made a film called *bambi*.
10. eskimos train dogs to pull sleds.

# Chapter 21

# Using Punctuation Marks

When you talk, you usually pause at the end of a thought. If you ask a question, you raise your voice at the end of the sentence. You use your voice in other ways to help your listener understand you.

When you write, you cannot use your voice. However, there are marks that will help your reader understand you. The marks used in writing are called **punctuation marks.** They show where sentences end. They help to separate ideas. They point out questions and other kinds of sentences.

In this chapter, you will learn to use punctuation marks correctly. Then your writing will be clear. Your readers will be able to understand everything you write.

# 1 The Period

> A **period (.)** is used after sentences, initials, and abbreviations.

**1. Use a period at the end of a statement or a command.** The period tells you the sentence has ended. If you read the sentence aloud, your voice stays the same or goes down at the end.

**Statement:** I like mystery stories.
**Command:** Return all library books.

**2. Use a period after an initial.** The period tells you that the single letter stands for a whole name.

Martha D. Washington      E. B. White

**3. Use a period after most abbreviations.** Days, months, streets, titles in names, and other words have abbreviations. Here are some examples.

| Streets and Places | | Measures | |
|---|---|---|---|
| Street | St. | inch | in. |
| Road | Rd. | foot | ft. |
| Avenue | Ave. | mile | mi. |
| Place | Pl. | pound | lb. |
| Boulevard | Blvd. | ounce | oz. |
| South | S. *or* So. | pint | pt. |
| Post Office | P.O. | quart | qt. |
| Company | Co. | gallon | gal. |

| Day and Months | | Names | |
|---|---|---|---|
| Monday | Mon. ✓ | Mister | Mr. ✓ |
| Saturday | Sat. | Mistress | Mrs. |
| January | Jan. | Doctor | Dr. |
| September | Sept. | (no long form) | Ms. |

Some abbreviations do not need periods.

| gram | g | liter | l |
|---|---|---|---|
| meter | m | Zone Improvement Plan | ZIP |

## Exercises  Using the Period Correctly

**A.** Write the following word groups, or phrases. Use periods where they are needed.

1. Dr Patel
2. U S Grant
3. The Marshall Co
4. 6 lb
5. Beech St
6. Wed, Feb 2
7. P O Box 16
8. Mayfield Rd
9. Ms Carter
10. 4 oz

**B.** Write the following sentences. Use periods correctly.

1. Our new mail carrier is Ms Baldwin
2. Mr Nimitz fixed the scoreboard
3. A A Milne wrote about Christopher Robin
4. Sam Evans, Jr is my dad's name
5. Tell me about Susan B Anthony
6. Write your ZIP code clearly
7. Dr J Salk found a way to prevent polio
8. Mrs Harris is a piano tuner
9. Watch Ms Ramos lead the jazz band
10. Thomas A Edison invented the electric light

# 2 The Question Mark

> A **question mark (?)** is used at the end of every question.

The following sentences are questions. They end with **question marks**. When you read these sentences aloud, your voice goes up at the end.

Are you going for a walk?
May I come too?

## Exercise  Using the Question Mark Correctly

Write the following sentences. Some are statements. Some are commands. Some are questions. Use the correct end mark for each sentence.

1. Will the volcano erupt again
2. Have you seen Cara's coin collection
3. My finger got stuck in the glue
4. Please count your change
5. Be careful with the fish bowl
6. How far away is the moon
7. I heard the whistle of the train
8. Ronald stood on his head
9. Put the guppies in the bowl
10. Where does your cat sleep

# 3 The Exclamation Point

> An **exclamation point (!)** is used at the end of exclamations.

An exclamation shows surprise, anger, fright, or other strong feeling. It ends with an **exclamation point.** An exclamation point may replace a period after a statement or command that shows strong feeling.

When you read exclamations aloud, let your voice show feeling.

> How cold this water is!
> Don't open that door!

## Exercise  Using the Exclamation Point Correctly

Write these sentences, using correct end marks. All four kinds of sentences are included. Read each sentence aloud. Let your voice tell listeners what kind each sentence is.

1. A comet was named for Edmund Halley
2. Beatrix Potter wrote about rabbits
3. When do astronauts sleep
4. What a strange fish a seahorse is
5. Do you know a poem by Gwendolyn Brooks
6. Felipe doesn't need crutches any more
7. Don't drop the ball
8. How dangerous that stunt is
9. Do dolphins have a language of their own
10. What a terrible forest fire that was

# 4 The Comma

> A **comma (,)** is used in writing dates, addresses, parts of letters, and series.
>
> If you are reading aloud, a comma is a clue telling you to stop briefly. It is not an end mark.

**1. In writing dates, use a comma between the day and the year.**

July 4, 1776

The Brooklyn Bridge opened on May 24, 1883.

**2. In writing addresses, use a comma between the city and the state.**

Atlanta, Georgia

The Alamo is in San Antonio, Texas.

**3. In a friendly letter, use a comma after the greeting and after the closing.**

*Dear Ms. Silver,*   *Yours truly,*

**4. In a series of three or more persons or things, use a comma to separate them.**

The singers are Eddie, Valerie, and Ann.

**Exercises**  **Using the Comma Correctly**

**A.** Write the following sentences. Use commas where they are needed.

1. Alexander Graham Bell made the first telephone call on March 10 1876.
2. Boys Town is near Omaha Nebraska.
3. No other American city is further north than Barrow Alaska.
4. Can you draw circles squares and triangles?
5. Hawaii became a state on August 21 1959.
6. The steamboat sailed to Albany New York.
7. Pioneers found prairies deserts and mountains.
8. This century will end on December 31 1999.
9. There is a diamond mine in Murfreesboro Arkansas.
10. You need wood paper and glue to make a kite.

**B.** Write this friendly letter. Fill in today's date. Use commas correctly.

_____<br>(date)

Dear Jamie

   Our family just came back from a trip. We visited an old mine near Phoenix Arizona. I picked up some rocks. I think they have gold silver and copper in them. I will save one for you.

Your friend<br>Beverly

# 5 More About the Comma

> A **comma** is used to set off quotations. It is also used to set off the name of a person spoken to, and after *yes* and *no* at the beginning of a sentence.

**1. Use a comma to set off a direct quotation from the rest of the sentence.** A direct quotation means the exact words a person says. The quotation marks go at the beginning and end of the words being said. Always place the comma before the quotation marks.

> Gloria said, "My pencil is broken."
> "You may use mine," Jonah said.

**2. Use a comma after *yes* or *no* at the beginning of a sentence.**

> Yes, the bus was on time.
> No, New Orleans does not get much snow.

**3. Use a comma after the name of a person spoken to.**

> Robin, can you play soccer today?
> Gerry, I found your violin case.

**Key to Writing** Use commas to keep your ideas clear. For example, notice how commas make this sentence mean two different things.

> Marc, Dad, and I are planning to visit Missouri.
> Marc, Dad and I are planning to visit Missouri.

# Exercises  Using the Comma Correctly

**A.** Write the following sentences. Use commas where they are needed.

1. Yes I can work a computer.
2. Ralph said "The moon circles the earth."
3. "Come and see the rainbow" Gina called.
4. Frank it's your turn to keep score.
5. "Yes there are buds on the trees" Ingrid said.
6. The genie said "You may have three wishes."
7. No my brother cannot run as fast as I can.
8. Jo asked "Can windmills turn without wind?"
9. The director said "Alfred open the curtain."
10. Tigers lions and panthers are all cats.

**B.** Write the following fable. Nine commas are missing. Use commas where they are needed.

"I am stronger than you" said the sun. "No you are not" answered the wind. The sun said "I will prove it. You try to make that traveler remove his coat." The wind said "That's easy."

"Whoosh" exclaimed the wind. The traveler wrapped his coat tighter. The wind blew harder. The traveler held his coat closer. "Sun you try" said the tired wind. The sun smiled and came out. "It is getting hot" the traveler sighed as he removed his coat.

# 6 The Apostrophe

> The **apostrophe** (') is used in possessive nouns and in contractions.

**1. Use an apostrophe in possessive nouns.**

To make a singular noun show possession, add an apostrophe and an *s*.

Kathy's dog     artist's brush

If a plural noun does not end in *s*, add an apostrophe and an *s* to show possession.

women's coats     men's hats

If a plural noun ends in *s*, add only an apostrophe.

clowns' tricks     bears' dens

**2. Use an apostrophe in contractions.** A contraction is a word formed by putting together two words. Some letters of the original word are left out. The apostrophe shows where letters are left out.

| | | | |
|---|---|---|---|
| I am | I'm | is not | isn't |
| you are | you're | would not | wouldn't |
| he is | he's | should not | shouldn't |
| she will | she'll | have not | haven't |
| it is | it's | has not | hasn't |
| they are | they're | do not | don't |

## Exercises   Using the Apostrophe Correctly

**A.** Write the following phrases. Use apostrophes correctly to make every underlined noun show possession.

1. Albertos house
2. a flys buzz
3. all foxes tails
4. Dianes turn
5. two students books
6. Mothers job
7. the Johnsons car
8. my uncles whistle
9. the kittens purr
10. childrens voices

**B.** Write these sentences. Change each of the underlined phrases to a contraction.

1. Mona should not dive off the board.
2. I will show you how the engine works.
3. You are going to see the first spaceship.
4. The panda would not let them see her cub.
5. He is training for the Olympics.
6. She will rescue the cat in the tree.
7. Adam is not sure his kite will fly.
8. I will not tell you about the surprise.
9. We are building a model of Ft. Dearborn.
10. Do not forget to call your grandfather.

**C.** Rewrite the following paragraph. Change the underlined words to possessives or contractions.

   Moms washing machine does not work. My sister Janes gym shorts are not clean. "Can not you wear your jeans?" Mom asked. "I will ask the gym teacher in class today," answered Jane.

# 7 Quotation Marks

> **Quotation marks** (" ") are used to set off direct quotations. They are also used around titles of poems, stories, and reports.

**1. Use quotation marks to set off direct quotations.** Use quotation marks before and after the words a person says. Use a comma to set off a direct quotation. Always place the comma before the quotation mark.

"Dinosaurs were the largest animals," Dan said.
Lee said, "Dinosaurs were larger than whales."

**2. Use quotation marks around titles of poems, stories, and reports.**

"Simple Simon"   "Cinderella"   "Farm Tools"

## Exercise   Using Quotation Marks Correctly

Write these sentences. Use quotation marks correctly.

1. This rock is sandstone, said Miss Vila.
2. Victor called his report Spinning Spiders.
3. Is the tale Sleeping Beauty in this book?
4. Terence said, Pigs are very smart.
5. The poem The Star is also a song.
6. We acted out The Lion and the Mouse.
7. Bianca asked, Did they find the treasure?
8. Our class liked the report Space Visitors.
9. I figured out the code! shouted Toru.
10. My cat's name comes from the poem Moon.

# 8 Writing Book Titles

> Underline titles of books. Follow the rules for capitalizing words in titles.

Book titles are underlined when they are written.

*The 500 Hats of Bartholomew Cubbins*

In books, these titles are printed in italic letters.

*The 500 Hats of Bartholomew Cubbins*

## Exercises  Writing Titles Correctly

**A.** Write these titles. Use quotation marks or underlining.

Examples: <u>The Sun</u> (book)  "Moochie" (poem)

1. Homer Price (book)
2. Reflections (poem)
3. Ghost Stories (book)
4. The Camel (poem)
5. Windy Nights (poem)
6. The Hungry Thing (book)
7. The Grasshopper (poem)
8. Is Anyone Here? (book)
9. Madeline's Rescue (book)
10. Thumbprint (poem)

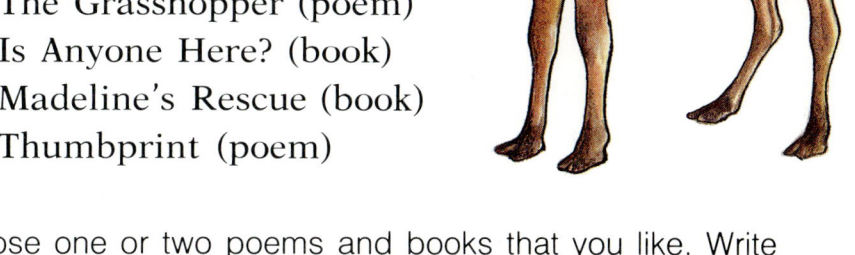

**B.** Choose one or two poems and books that you like. Write their titles. Tell what each one is about.

# Exercises for Mastery   Chapter 21

## Using Punctuation Marks

**A. Using the Period Correctly** Write these word groups. Use periods where they are needed.

1. Mr Chen
2. Aug 18
3. 1 ft 2 in
4. Erie Blvd
5. P O Box 53
6. 4 gal
7. New Shoelace Co
8. Joseph Addison, Jr
9. Mrs Jackson
10. E Ninth St

**B. Using End Marks Correctly** Write the correct end marks for these sentences.

1. What a great skater Dorothy is
2. Steve threw a coin in the wishing well
3. Does a submarine have windows
4. Watch out for that ball
5. How smooth the snake's skin is

**C. Using the Comma Correctly** Write the following letter. Use commas where they are needed.

                              _____
                                   (date)

Dear Grandpa

   Do you remember when we got our dog Punch? It was on May 8 1986. Punch still likes to run jump and play. He obeys when I say "Stay!" We took Punch to Cairo Illinois.

                              Love
                              Heather

**D. Using the Apostrophe Correctly** Number your paper from 1 to 10. Change each underlined word or phrase to either the possessive form or a contraction.

1. <u>You are</u> a good drummer.
2. This is <u>Juanitas</u> magic set.
3. The <u>monsters</u> eye is yellow.
4. This soap <u>will not</u> make bubbles.
5. The goose <u>would not</u> help the red hen.
6. I borrowed <u>Alberts</u> tub to bathe the dog.
7. Dale <u>has not</u> got a football helmet.
8. <u>It is</u> cold on the desert at night.
9. Pony Express <u>riders</u> horses were fast.
10. <u>Emmas</u> camera has a flash bulb.

**E. Using Quotation Marks Correctly** Write the following sentences. Use quotation marks where they are needed.

1. Todd said, Follow the footprints.
2. Maris read The Brave Little Tailor twice.
3. The poem Eletelephony has mixed-up words.
4. Dorothy said, I want to go back to Kansas.
5. Hansel and Gretel is a famous fairy tale.

**F. Writing Titles Correctly** Write these titles. Use quotation marks or underlining where each is needed.

1. Caps for Sale (book)
2. The Real Princess (story)
3. Encyclopedia Brown (book)
4. The Grasshopper (poem)
5. Away Went Wolfgang (book)

# Using Grammar in Writing

**A.** Red Riding Hood said to the wolf, "What a big nose you have, Grandmother!" The sentence in this quotation is an exclamation. Many stories have sentences like this. Choose a story. Write the title. Tell part of the story in one or two paragraphs. Try to use all four kinds of sentences.

**B.** You are a scientist. Suddenly you hear a strange voice on your radio. The voice is coming from outer space. Have a conversation with the voice. Write your conversation. Use commas and quotation marks correctly.

**C. Using Punctuation in Math** Collect several empty milk cartons or bottles of different sizes. Read the label on each container. The label tells how much each one holds. Look for containers that hold a gallon, a half gallon, a quart, and a pint.

Fill the largest one with water. Pour the water into the smaller ones to answer these questions. For example, how many quarts fill one gallon? Write your answers. Use abbreviations correctly.

1 gal. = \_\_?\_\_ qt.
1 gal. = \_\_?\_\_ pt.
½ gal. = \_\_?\_\_ qt.
½ gal. = \_\_?\_\_ pt.
1 qt. = \_\_?\_\_ pt.

# Chapter 21 Review

**A. Using Punctuation Marks** Write these sentences. Add periods, ending marks, commas, and quotation marks where they are needed.

1. Will this caterpillar become a butterfly
2. What a busy airport O'Hare is
3. The emperor said  The clothes fit well
4. Mr P T Barnum owned the circus
5. Wool comes from sheep goats and camels
6. Do you know what happened on May 5 1961
7. How quickly the squirrel climbed the tree
8. A riverboat museum is in Dubuque Iowa
9. Mt. Fujiyama is in Japan Ms Stone said
10. Ava picked up the pins tacks and coins

**B. Using Apostrophes and Writing Titles Correctly** Write the following sentences. Add quotation marks and apostrophes where needed. Underline titles as necessary.

1. The Dream is a poem that doesnt rhyme.
2. Alan gave me the book Space.
3. Baba Yaga is a Russian folk tale.
4. Beths class learned the poem The Tiger.
5. The Coconut Thieves is a tale from Africa.
6. Ezra Jack Keats wrote the book The Snowy Day.
7. Evitas sister likes the poem The Bat.
8. Magic Key is a story Erics mother read.
9. Vincents book Pinocchio has pictures.
10. The poem Pigeon People has nice rhythm.

# Cumulative Review

Unit 4

## Composition

**A. Understanding a Report** Read this paragraph from a report. Write it with the changes that are marked. Then answer the questions.

¶ the tiniest horses in the world are shetland ponies⊙ Many are less than three ft. high. these shaggy ponies are little but very strong⊙ I've always wanted a pony. Shetland ponies have worked on farms and ^in coal mines.

1. What is the main idea of the paragraph?
2. Write two facts about Shetland ponies.
3. Name a kind of work Shetlands have done.

**B. Writing Letters** Write an invitation to a friend or relative. Invite the person to your class play. Include all five parts of a letter. Be sure the information is clear.

## Grammar

**Capital Letters and Punctuation Marks** Write these sentences correctly.

1. separate the pennies nickels and dimes
2. summer starts in december in brazil
3. miners hats have lights on them
4. submarines can go very deep lila said
5. did dr. Garbers nurse weigh you

6. we rode a bus through the san diego zoo
7. what a big bumblebee
8. women could not vote until august 26 1920
9. edward read the book <u>trouble for trumpets</u>
10. ms kearns said wear a cap in the pool

## Related Skills

**A. Using the Library** Answer the questions below.

1. Are reference books fiction or nonfiction?
2. Are fiction books arranged by title or author in the library?
3. The card catalog has author, title, and subject cards. What kind of cards would help you find books about icebergs?
4. Where do you find the index of a book? Where is the table of contents?
5. What letter would you look under in the encyclopedia to find an article about Admiral Richard Byrd?

**B. Thinking Clearly** Read the unfair generalizations below. Rewrite them. Change words to make each generalization fair.

1. All Americans love baseball.
2. It never snows in Florida.
3. Beverly Cleary is the best children's author.
4. Goldfish always make good pets.
5. Science is everyone's favorite subject.

# POWER HANDBOOK

**Guides for the Process of Writing**    330–332

**Topics for Writing**    333–335

**Guide to Spelling**    336–340

**Word Bank for Writers**    341–347

# Guides for the Process of Writing

## Prewriting

1. Choose a topic. It should not be too big to write about.
2. Write notes about your topic. Write everything that comes to your mind.
3. Study your notes. Decide what your main idea will be.
4. Cross out any ideas that are not about the main idea. Add any new ideas you think of.
5. Put your notes in an order that makes sense.

## Writing a Draft

1. Write a topic sentence about your main idea.
2. Use your notes to write sentences about your topic.

## Revising

Read your draft. Think about these questions to make it better. Mark any changes. Use the marks on page 331.

1. Is your writing interesting? Did you write a good beginning and ending sentence?
2. Does every sentence tell about the main idea?
3. Should anything be taken out or added?
4. Are your sentences in an order that makes sense?
5. Is every sentence a complete thought?
6. Have you used the best words to tell your ideas?

## Proofreading

Read your draft again. These questions will help you to find mistakes in capital letters, punctuation, and spelling. You can also see what chapters to look in for help.

1. Is every word group a sentence? (Chapter 4)
2. Does every sentence begin with a capital letter? (Chapters 4, 20)
3. Are all proper nouns capitalized? (Chapters 6, 20)
4. Does every sentence have the correct end mark? (Chapters 4, 21)
5. Do you need to add commas, apostrophes, quotation marks, or underlining? (Chapter 21)
6. Is each word spelled correctly? Did you look up words you are not sure of in the dictionary? (Chapter 3)

**Marks for Revising and Proofreading Your Writing**

| Mark | Meaning | Example |
|---|---|---|
| ≡ | Capitalize a letter. | Paul adams |
| ⊙ | Put in a period. | a trip⊙ Her coat |
| ∧ | Add words. | come ∧to school |
| — | Take out words. | saw a ~~a~~ kite |
| / | Use lowercase. | my best /Friend |
| ∧ | Add a comma. | cats∧ dogs∧ and birds |
| ¶ | Begin a new paragraph. | rain.¶ The next day |

Guides for the Process of Writing

## Preparing Your Final Copy

1. Make a clean copy of your writing. Be sure you made all the changes you marked on your draft.
2. Did you indent your paragraphs?
3. Is your handwriting neat and easy to read? This chart shows the correct way to write cursive letters.

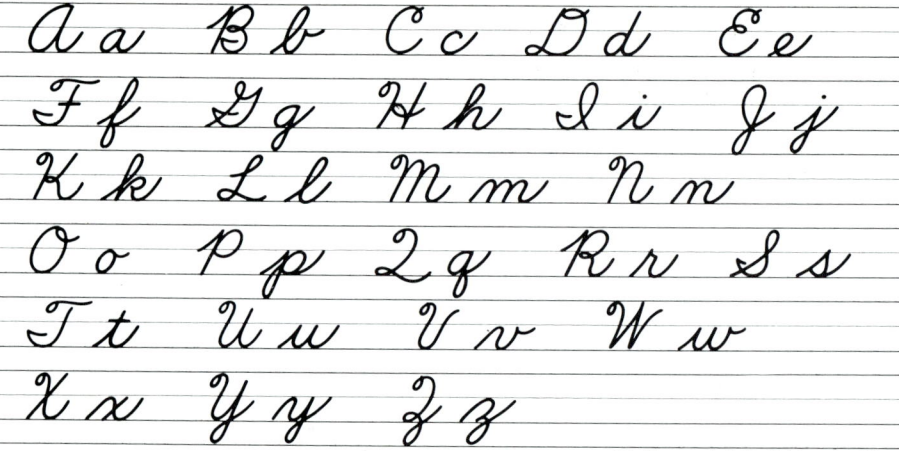

McDougal, Littell Handwriting

## Sharing Your Writing

Choose a way to share your writing. You may trade your work with a friend. You may read your writing to your classmates or hang it on the bulletin board. Perhaps you would like to start a book of things you have written. Think of other ways to share your writing.

# Topics for Writing

Here are some ideas for topics to write about. You may choose one or use these ideas to brainstorm. That will lead you to a main idea to write about.

## Journal Starters

1. What I like best about myself
2. A cartoon story of a recent event
3. How I would spend $1,000
4. My earliest memory
5. Jobs I do at home
6. What I love and what I hate
7. What I do on Saturday
8. How I got my name and what it means
9. My friends and why they like me
10. If I were like Superman or Superwoman

## General Topics for Paragraphs

1. Someone I would like to meet
2. A dream I remember
3. What to do on a rainy day
4. Staying overnight at a friend's house
5. A ride on an elephant (camel, mule)
6. My wish book
7. A pillow fight
8. My dog can count (sing, talk)
9. The tree that grows money
10. How I make my parents proud

Topics for Writing

## Topics for Stories

1. The time I forgot the tickets
2. The ghost that sings at midnight
3. The case of the missing gold coin
4. Searching for a lost pet
5. My talking clock takes over
6. Giving or getting a surprise party
7. What happened when I didn't keep my promise
8. The day I got lost In the store
9. A flying car to the rescue
10. Everybody knew except me

## Topics for a Descriptive Paragraph

1. An enchanted castle
2. A family of lions
3. A circus performer
4. A giant's house
5. A knight in armor
6. A clock
7. A bus
8. A pirate ship
9. A storm
10. A peacock

## Topics for a Paragraph That Tells How

Explain how to . . .

1. Use a compass
2. Ride a skateboard
3. Make a diorama
4. Take a picture
5. Bathe a dog
6. Build an igloo
7. Make a scrapbook
8. Start an aquarium
9. Throw a boomerang
10. Do a magic trick

## Topics for a Report

1. A famous explorer (inventor, scientist)
2. Animals of the Arctic (forest, desert)
3. A planet (the moon, the sun)
4. A career in television (announcer, camera operator)
5. An Indian tribe (Hopi, Seminole)
6. Volcanoes (tornados, hurricanes)
7. Crocodiles (alligators, snakes)
8. Inside a pyramid (cave, coal mine)
9. The ships that Columbus (Pilgrims) sailed
10. Children of Japan (Kenya, Mexico)

Topics for Writing

# Guide to Spelling

## How To Improve Your Spelling

You can learn to spell well. These guides will help you to improve your spelling skills.

### Look at words carefully.

When you come to a new word, look at it carefully. Some words, like *February,* are tricky. Practice looking at every letter of new or tricky words. Write the words several times.

### Pronounce words correctly.

People often misspell words because they say them wrong. For example, you may write *hunderd* for *hundred* if you are not pronouncing it correctly.

### Study words that you have trouble spelling.

Keep a list of words you often misspell. Add any new words you learn to your list. Study the list until you can spell them correctly. Use the study method on the next page.

### Use clues to remember words that are hard to spell.

Think of a clue to help you remember how to spell a word. For example, to help you remember how to spell *country,* remember the sentence, "Your country can *count* on you!"

### Proofread your writing.

Always reread your written work. Look at every word. If you are not sure if a word is spelled correctly, look it up in the dictionary.

## Steps for Learning New Words

Study any word that gives you trouble. If you learn to spell it correctly, you will not have to correct it again. Here are some steps that will help you to spell words correctly.

**1. Look at the word.**
Study each letter. Try to remember the way the word looks when it is spelled correctly.

**2. Say the word.**
Pronounce it carefully. Do not leave out any part of the word.

**3. Copy the word.**
Be sure you copy every letter in correct order.

**4. Close your eyes. Think of the word.**
Try to see it in your mind.

**5. Spell the word aloud. Do not look at it.**
Imagine you are writing the word as you spell.

**6. Next, write the word.**
Write clearly and neatly.

**7. Then, check what you have written.**
Did you spell the word correctly? If you did, write it once more. If you did not, repeat the steps until you can spell the word correctly.

## Rules for Spelling

If you remember certain rules, it will help you to spell correctly.

### Adding Suffixes to Words Ending in Silent e

A **suffix** is a word part added to the ending of a word. When you add a suffix that begins with a vowel to a word ending in silent e, you usually drop the final e.

    dance + er = dancer
    bake + ed = baked
    wise + est = wisest
    take + ing = taking

### Adding Suffixes to Words Ending in y

Sometimes you add a suffix to a word that ends with y following a consonant. In this case, you usually change the y to i. You do not change the y when the ending ing is added.

    carry + ed = carried
    happy + er = happier
    lucky + est = luckiest
    merry + ly = merrily
    fly + ing = flying

### Doubling the Final Consonant

When a word ends in a single consonant after a single short vowel, double the final consonant. Then add the ending.

    nap + ed = napped
    shop + er = shopper
    big + est = biggest
    mop + ing = mopping

## Spelling Words with *ie* and *ei*

Remember this rhyme to help you with *ie* and *ei* words.

> *i* before *e*
> Except after *c*
> Or when sounded as *a*
> As in *neighbor* or *weigh.*

These words follow the rules in the rhyme.

> *i* before *e*: *piece, brief*
> Except after *c*: *receive, ceiling*
> Or when sounded as *a*: *reindeer, eight*

These words do not follow the rule: *either, neither*

## Homophones: Words Often Confused

Words that sound the same or nearly the same are called **homophones.** They have different meanings and are usually spelled differently.

Here are some homophones that are used often. Learn what they are so you will use the words correctly.

### Here and Hear

*Here* means "in this place."
Put the money *here*.

*Hear* means "to listen to."
Do you *hear* the dial tone?

### Its and It's

*Its* means "belonging to it."
The rabbit wiggled *its* nose.

*It's* means "it is" or "it has."
*It's* going to eat a carrot. (It is)
*It's* never tried to run away. (It has)

### Right and Write

*Right* means "correct" or "the opposite of left."
Be sure to use the *right* key. (correct)
Don throws with his *right* hand. (opposite of left)

*Write* means "to form words with a pen or pencil."
Enid likes to *write* with a pen.

### There, Their, and They're

*There* means "at that place."
Hit the ball *there*.

*Their* means "belonging to them."
*Their* names are on *their* shirts.

*They're* means "they are."
*They're* wearing shoulder pads.

### To, Too, and Two

*To* means "in the direction of."
Go back *to* the starting point.

*Too* means also or very.
You went *too* fast.

*Two* is the number between one and three.
Move up *two* spaces.

### Your and You're

*Your* means "belonging to you."
*Your* key chain is broken.

*You're* means "you are."
*You're* going to lose your keys.

# Word Bank for Writers

Use these lists of words when you write. They will help you to make your writing interesting.

## Words To Name People, Places, and Things

### People—Jobs and Careers

| | |
|---|---|
| baker | mail carrier |
| ballplayer | mechanic |
| bus driver | nurse |
| computer programmer | pilot |
| | police officer |
| cook | salesperson |
| dancer | scientist |
| dentist | secretary |
| doctor | teacher |
| firefighter | veterinarian |
| lawyer | writer |

### Places and Buildings

| | |
|---|---|
| airport | market |
| apartment | museum |
| bus station | neighborhood |
| city | office |
| country | park |
| factory | restaurant |
| farm | skyscraper |
| library | theater |

### Names of Animal Groups

| Animals | Group Name |
|---|---|
| bees | swarm |
| birds | flock |
| elephants | herd |
| fish | school |
| geese | gaggle |
| lions | pride |
| wolves | pack |

### Seasons and Months

| **winter** | **summer** |
|---|---|
| December | June |
| January | July |
| February | August |
| **spring** | **fall** |
| March | September |
| April | October |
| May | November |

## Words To Describe People, Places, and Things

### Words That Show Feeling

| | |
|---|---|
| angry | nervous |
| anxious | joyful |
| bored | mean |
| calm | proud |
| frightened | relaxed |
| glad | sad |
| happy | thrilled |
| miserable | worried |

### Words That Show Shape

| | |
|---|---|
| circle | oval |
| cone | pointed |
| crooked | rectangle |
| cube | round |
| curve | square |
| flat | straight |
| lumpy | triangle |

### Words That Show Size

| | |
|---|---|
| enormous | skinny |
| huge | small |
| large | stout |
| little | tall |
| long | thin |
| narrow | tiny |
| short | wide |

### Color Words

**Red**
- cherry
- coral
- crimson
- pink
- rose
- ruby

**Green**
- emerald
- kelly
- lime
- mint
- moss
- olive

**Blue**
- aqua
- navy
- turquoise

**Orange**
- peach
- pumpkin
- tangerine

**Yellow**
- cream
- gold
- lemon
- mustard

**White**
- ivory
- milk
- pearl
- snow

**Brown**
- bronze
- chocolate
- walnut

**Black**
- coal
- ebony
- jet

*Word Bank for Writers*

## Sense Words

**Sight**

| | |
|---|---|
| bright | hazy |
| clear | pale |
| dark | shadowy |
| dim | shimmery |
| flashing | shining |
| fuzzy | sparkling |

**Sound**

| | |
|---|---|
| bang | hush |
| bark | peep |
| boom | roar |
| buzz | rumble |
| chime | scream |
| clink | sigh |
| crackle | slam |
| crash | squeal |
| hiss | whisper |
| hum | whistle |

**Taste**

| | |
|---|---|
| bitter | sour |
| mild | spicy |
| oily | strong |
| salty | sweet |

**Touch**

| | |
|---|---|
| bumpy | sandy |
| cold | silky |
| cool | slippery |
| damp | smooth |
| furry | soft |
| hairy | sticky |
| hard | velvety |
| hot | warm |
| rough | wet |

**Smell**

| | |
|---|---|
| clean | musty |
| damp | rotten |
| fishy | sharp |
| fresh | smoky |
| moldy | sweet |

Word Bank for Writers

# Words from Different Subjects

## Art

| | |
|---|---|
| artist | model |
| canvas | mural |
| carve | pastel |
| easel | portrait |
| landscape | sketch |
| mobile | style |

## Health

| | |
|---|---|
| blood | medicine |
| bone | minerals |
| brain | muscle |
| diet | nerve |
| disease | sight |
| exercise | skeleton |
| germs | stomach |
| hearing | tissue |
| heart | tonsils |
| height | vitamin |
| lungs | weight |

## Math

| | |
|---|---|
| addend | metric |
| addition | multiply |
| calendar | numeral |
| decimal | pint |
| divide | pound |
| fraction | problem |
| inch | product |
| gallon | quart |
| gram | remainder |
| hundred | segment |
| kilometer | subtract |
| liter | temperature |
| measure | thousand |
| meter | yard |

## Music

| | |
|---|---|
| accent | oboe |
| chord | perform |
| chorus | piano |
| compose | rhythm |
| drums | scale |
| flute | tempo |
| guitar | trombone |
| harmony | trumpet |
| harp | violin |
| melody | woodwind |

## Physical Education

| | |
|---|---|
| balance | pitcher |
| bounce | pivot |
| cartwheel | relay |
| crawl | signal |
| dive | somersault |
| dodge | stretch |
| double | tackle |
| dribble | triple |
| guard | tumbling |
| hitter | volley |

## Reading

| | |
|---|---|
| alphabet | poetry |
| capital | predicate |
| character | question |
| comma | revise |
| compound | rhyme |
| consonant | setting |
| describe | subject |
| fact | statement |
| idea | syllable |
| letter | topic |
| meaning | vowel |

## Science

| | |
|---|---|
| atom | mammal |
| axle | orbit |
| carbon | planet |
| chemical | pulley |
| energy | revolve |
| friction | rotate |
| gear | solar |
| insect | vapor |
| lava | volcano |
| machine | wildlife |

## Social Studies

| | |
|---|---|
| atlas | liberty |
| citizen | location |
| climate | mountain |
| community | nation |
| continent | ocean |
| customs | peace |
| discovery | pioneer |
| freedom | prairie |
| government | resource |
| island | river |

## Synonyms for Common Words

| | | |
|---|---|---|
| **ask** | invite | We cannot *invite* many people. |
| | question | *Question* the firefighters about their jobs. |
| | request | Please *request* the band to play a march. |
| **beautiful** | fair | The prince married the *fair* maiden. |
| | lovely | A rainbow is a *lovely* sight. |
| | pretty | That peacock has a *pretty* tail. |
| **big** | giant | They saw *giant* footprints in the sand. |
| | great | The play was a *great* success. |
| | huge | A *huge* rock blocked the cave. |
| **go (fast)** | chase | A fox will *chase* after a rabbit. |
| | hurry | *Hurry* outside to see the falling star. |
| | race | Brad had to *race* for third base. |
| | speed | The cars *speed* across the track. |
| **go (slow)** | crawl | Caterpillars *crawl* across the leaves. |
| | creep | Cats can *creep* without a sound. |
| | plod | The hikers had to *plod* through the mud. |
| **good** | excellent | Goats are *excellent* climbers. |
| | kind | A *kind* woman cared for the wounded bird. |
| | useful | A lever is a *useful* tool. |
| | wonderful | That movie was *wonderful*. |
| **hit** | bump | Klaus *bumped* his knee on the desk. |
| | knock | Susan *knocked* all the bottles down. |
| | strike | *Strike* that nail again. |

| | | |
|---|---|---|
| **hold** | grab<br>grip<br>keep | Do not *grab* the dog's tail.<br>*Grip* the bat with both hands.<br>*Keep* the ladder steady. |
| **laugh** | chuckle<br>giggle | Grandfather *chuckles* when I tell a joke.<br>We *giggle* when we watch the monkeys. |
| **like** | enjoy<br>love<br>prefer | Did Fern *enjoy* the speedboat ride?<br>Tom *loves* to make up riddles.<br>Martha *prefers* the top bunk. |
| **say<br>(loudly)** | cry<br>scream<br>shout | Abel *cried,* "The boat is sinking!"<br>"Head for the bridge," the guide *screamed.*<br>"Come down from the tree," Dana *shouted.* |
| **say<br>(quietly)** | mutter<br>whisper | "This lid is stuck," Leon *muttered.*<br>"We are going to surprise Mom,"<br>Angie *whispered.* |
| **see** | observe<br>sight<br>view | Lisa *observed* a ring around the moon.<br>The sailor *sighted* the raft.<br>Andrew *viewed* the race from the hill. |
| **wait** | remain<br>stay | The audience *remained* in their seats.<br>Jorge *stayed* in the locker room. |
| **walk** | hike<br>march<br>stroll | The scouts *hiked* along the trail.<br>The team *marched* into the stadium.<br>The clowns *strolled* among the crowd. |

**Word Bank for Writers**

# Index

*A, an, the,* 179, 186
Abbreviations
  in addresses, 298–299
  capital letters in, 296–297
  list of common, 310–311
  periods with, 310–311
Action verbs, 130, 132
Addresses, 248–249
  capital letters in, 298–299
  commas in, 314–315, 322, 325
  for envelopes, 248–249
Adjectives, 173–182
  *a, an,* and *the,* 179, 186
  comparison with, 180–182
  in descriptive writing, 174, 177–178, 188, 341
  kinds of, 176–178
  using, 174–175, 186
Adverbs, 183–185
  adding *-ly* to adjectives to form, 184
  list of common, 184
  using, 183, 185, 187–199
Advertisements, generalizations in 264
Alphabetical order
  arrangement of books in library, 270–271, 278
  card catalog cards, 272–273
  dictionary words, 34–35
  encyclopedia articles, 276–277
  index of books, 275
  in telephone book, 35
Antonyms, 42–43
Apostrophe
  in contractions, 144–146, 318–319
  with *it's,* 108–109, 111
  in possessive nouns, 92–93, 318–319
  in possessive pronouns, 106–109
Articles. See *A, an, the.*
Author, 270, 274
Author card, 272–273, 279

*Be,* forms of, 130–132, 140
Biography, 278
Body of friendly letter, 245–247
Book report, 292
Books
  encyclopedias, 276–277
  fiction, 270–271
  finding, in library, 270–271
  index, 274–275
  nonfiction, 270–271
  parts of, 274–275
  reference, 270–271
  sharing with others, 278, 292
  table of contents, 274–275
  title page, 274–275
  titles of, 271–272, 302–303
  writing a book report, 292
Borrowed words, 22–23, 31
Brainstorming, to get ideas in writing, 68–69, 161

Capital letters, 295–307
  of abbreviations, 296, 297
  in addresses, 298–299
  in greetings and closing of letters, 300–301
  *I,* 296–297
  of initials, 296–297
  in names, 296–299
  in outlines, 300–301
  in poetry lines, 300–301
  in quotations, 300–301
  in sentences, 52–53, 56–57, 61, 64, 300–301
  for titles
    in names, 296–297, 304
    of written works, 302–303
Card catalog, 272–273, 279
Characters
  in plays, 124, 164
  in stories, 116–119, 125, 156–157, 167

348

Class story, 122–123
Climax, of story, 116–117, 125
Clipped words, 24, 31
Closing of letter, 246–247, 300–301, 305, 314–315
Clues to meanings of words, 38–39, 44–45, 47
Comma
  in addresses, 314–315
  in dates, 314–315
  in letters, 314–315
  with name of person spoken to, 316–317
  in quotations, 316–317
  in series, 314–315
  after *yes* or *no*, 316–317
Commands, 52–53, 58, 61, 310–311
Commercials, generalizations in, 264
Common nouns, 88–89
Compound words, 25, 31
Concrete poem, 212
Contractions
  apostrophe in, 144–146, 147, 151, 318–319
  with negatives, 147, 151
Conversation, carrying on a, 10–11
Creative writing, 77, 165, 199, 235, 291
Cursive handwriting, 254, 332

Dates, commas in, 314–315
Decisions, making, 261, 266
Descriptions, 191–201
  paragraphs that describe, 192–200
  planning and writing, 194–197, 199
  sharing, 196–197
  words that describe, 194, 198
Dictionary, 33–47
  alphabetical order in, 34–35
  antonyms, 42–43
  definitions, 38–39
  entry words, 38–39
  guide words, 36–37
  homophones, 46
  synonyms, 40–41

Directions, 215–225
  emergency, 224
  giving, 216–217
  listening to oral, 220–221, 224
  reading and following, 218–219
  safety, 224
  in tests, 222–223
  written, 218–219, 222–223, 225
Draft, writing a
  description, 194–195
  *how* paragraph, 230–233
  paragraph, 70–71
  report, 286–288
  story, 161–163
Echoic words, 20–21, 31, 208–209
Editing. *See* Proofreading; Revising.
Encyclopedia, 261, 276–277
Ending marks of sentences. *See* Exclamation Point; Period; Question Mark.
English, Using in Other Subjects,
  art, 30
  cursive handwriting, 254
  drama, 124
  health and safety, 224, 236
  math, 266
  reading, 16, 292
  science, 78, 200
  social studies, 166, 278
  spelling, 46
Entry words, in dictionary, 38–39
Envelopes, addressing, 248–249, 298–299, 314–315
*-er*, (suffix), 28–29
Exclamation point, 52–53, 313,
Exclamations, 52–53, 61, 313
Explaining How. *See How* paragraph.

Fable, 116–117, 125
Facts
  in encyclopedias,
  finding, 261
  taking notes, 284–285
  and opinions, 258–262
Fiction books, 270–271
Friendly letters. *See* Letters, Friendly.

Generalizations, 263–267
Greeting, of letter, 244–245, 247, 301, 305, 314–315
Guides for
  class story, 123
  conversation, carrying on, 11
  description, revising, 196
  following written directions, 219
  helping people listen to you, 8
  *how* paragraph, revising, 232
  listening to directions, 221
  paragraph
    proofreading, 74
    revising, 72
  report, revising, 288
  story, revising, 162
  story, telling, 119
  talking on telephone, 13
  telling how, 234
Guide words, in dictionary, 36–37

Handbook. *See* Power Handbook.
Handwriting, cursive, 254, 332
*Has, have, had. See* Helping verbs.
Heading, of letter, 244, 247
Helping verbs, 133–135, 140–141, 142–143
Homophones, 46, 339–340
*How* paragraph, 227–237
  prewriting, 230–231
  proofreading, 237
  revising, 232–233
  sharing, 234
  signal words in, 233
  topic sentence for, 229, 237

*I*
  capitalization of, 296–297
  and *me*, 100–103
  as subject, 102–103
  verb forms with, 137
Imperative sentences. *See* Commands.
Indenting, in paragraph, 64–65, 246

*-ing*, verbs ending in, 133–135, 141, 149
Index, 274–275
Information
  finding in books, 270–273
  gathering for reports, 261, 284–285
  taking notes, 284–285
Initials, 296–297, 310–311
Interview, conducting, 290
Introductions, making, 6–7
Invitations, 250–251
*Is, are, am, was, were*, 130–132, 134, 140, 144–146
*Its* and *it's*, 108–109

Languages, words from other, 22–23
*-less* (suffix), 28–29
Letters, Friendly, 243–255
  capitalization in, 300–301
  envelopes, addressing. *See* Envelopes.
  invitations, 250–251
  parts of
    body, 245–247, 253
    closing, 246–247, 255, 300–301, 314–315
    greeting, 244, 247, 301, 314–315,
    heading, 244, 247
    signature, 246, 247
  thank-you notes, 252–253
Library, 269–279
  biographies, 278
  card catalog, 272–273
  fiction books, 270–273, 278
  nonfiction books, 270–273, 278
  reference books, 270–271
Listening skills. *See* Speaking and listening.
Literature. *See* Books; Fable, Poetry; Stories, telling; Stories, writing; Tall tale.

Main idea in paragraphs. *See* Paragraphs; Topic sentence.
Main verbs. *See* Verbs.
*Me*, 100–105

Messages, taking, 14–15
Modifiers. See Adjectives; Adverbs.
Moral, of a fable, 116–117

Names
   capitalization of, 296–297
Negatives, 147, 151
*No*-words, *not*-words. See Negatives.
Nonfiction books, 270–271
*Not*, in contractions, 145–147, 153, 318–319
Notes, taking for reports, 284–285
Nouns, 85–97
   common, 88–89
   plural, 90–91, 95, 190
   possessive forms of, 92–93, 95, 318–319
   in predicate of sentences, 86–87
   proper, 88–89, 94, 97, 296–299
   singular, 90–91, 95
   in subject of sentence, 86–87
n't. See *Not*, in contractions.

Object pronouns. See Pronouns used in other parts of the sentence.
Opinions
   and facts, 258–262
   forming, 260
   in generalizations, 263–265
Outlines, 286–287, 293, 300–301

Paragraphs, 63–79
   that describe, 77–78
   drafts of, 70–71
   indenting, 64–65
   main idea in, 64–67, 69, 286–288
   prewriting, 68–69, 75
   proofreading, 74–75
   revising, 72–73, 75
   sentences in, 64–67
   steps for writing, 75
   in stories, 158–159
   taking notes, 69, 290
   that tell how, 227
   topic sentence in, 66–67, 70–71, 75, 195

Parts of speech. See Adjectives; Adverbs; Nouns; Pronouns; Verbs.
Past forms of verbs, 139–141, 142–143
Period
   with abbreviations, 310–311
   after initials, 310–311
   at end of sentences, 52–53, 56–57, 64, 310–311
   in outlines, 286
Plays, 124, 164
Plural forms. See Nouns; Pronouns.
Poetry, 203–213
   capital letters in, 300–301
   concrete, 212
   echoic words in, 208–209
   feeling in, 205–206
   lines in, 204–205
   pictures in, 206–207
   rhyme, 208–209
   rhythm in, 210–211
   sounds in, 208–209
   stanza, 204–205
   writing, 207, 212
Possessive nouns, 92–93, 95, 318–319
Possessive pronouns, 106–109
Power Handbook, 329–347
Predicate, 54–55, 59
   noun in, 86–87
   verb in, 54, 128–129
   See also Verbs.
Prefixes, 26–27, 31
Present form of verbs, 136–138, 140, 149
Prewriting
   descriptive paragraphs, 68–69, 75
   guides in Handbook, 330
   *how* paragraphs, 230–231
   paragraphs, 68–69, 75
   reports, 284–285
   stories, 160–161
Process of Writing. See Draft, writing; Power Handbook; Prewriting; Proofreading; Revising.

Pronouns, 99–113
   in contractions, 108–109
   *I* and *me*, 100–105
   in other parts of the sentence, 104–105
   *its* and *it's*, 107, 108–109
   plural, 100–101
   possessive, 106–109
   singular, 100–101
   as subjects, 102–103
   *their*, *there*, and *they're*, 108–109
Proofreading
   marks for, 331
   paragraphs, 75
   reports, 288–289
Proper nouns, 88–89, 94, 97, 298–299
Punctuation marks, 309–325
     *See* Apostrophe; Comma; Exclamation Point; Period; Question mark; Quotation marks; Underlining.

Question mark, 52–53, 312
Questions, 52–53, 312
Quotation marks, 302–303, 320–321
Quotations
   capital letter for first word of, 300–301
   commas with, 316–317
   quotation marks with, 320

*re-* (prefix), 26–27
Reading aloud, 118–119
Reports, 281–293
   choosing a subject, 284–285
   drafts of, 286–287
   finishing, 289
   interview for, 290
   notes for, 284–285
   outline for, 286–287
   paragraphs in, 282–283, 288–289
   planning, 284–287
   prewriting, 284–285
   proofreading, 293, 331
   revising, 288–289, 330
   sharing, 289

Return address, 249, 298–299
Revising
   descriptions, 196–197
   explanations, 232–233
   marks used in (proofreading symbols), 331
   paragraphs, 72–73
   reports, 288–289
   stories, 162
Rhyme in poetry, 208–209
Rhythm in poetry, 210–211
Roman numerals, in outlines, 286–287
Run-on sentences, 56–57, 59

Sense words, 343
Sentences, 49–61
   capital letter for first word, 52–53, 56–57, 64, 300–301
   commands, 52–53, 61, 310–311
   end punctuation in, 310–313
   exclamations, 52–53, 58, 61, 313
   kinds of, 52–53, 58, 61
   parts of, 50, 54–55, 59
   predicate in, 50, 54–55, 59, 61, 128
   questions, 52–53, 312
   run-on, 56–57, 59
   statements, 52–53
   subject in, 50, 54–55, 59, 61, 128
   topic, 66–67, 195
Setting
   in plays, 124
   in stories, 156–157
Signature of letter, 246–247
Size words, 188, 193–194, 196, 212, 343
Speaking and listening skills, 5–17
   about a book, 16
   carrying on a conversation, 10–11
   giving directions, 216–217
   giving opinions, 262
   giving a puppet show, 164
   helping people listen, 8–9, 20, 50, 86, 174
   an interview, 290
   listening to directions, 220–221

listening for sounds, 198
making introductions, 6-7
reading aloud, 118-119
taking a message, 14-15
talking on the telephone, 12-13
telling a class story, 122-123
telling how, 234-235
telling stories about yourself, 120-121
Spelling
  guide to, 336-340
  homophones, 46, 339-340
Stanza, 204-205
Statements, 52-53, 61, 310-311
Stories, telling, 115-125
  characters in, 116-119
  class story, 122-123
  climax of, 116-117
  fable, 116-117, 125
  parts of, 116-117
  reading aloud, 118-119
  about yourself, 120-121
Stories, writing, 155-167
  characters in, 156-157, 161, 164
  parts of, 158-159, 161
  proofreading, 162-163
  revising, 162
  setting in, 156-161
  what happens in, 156-161
Study skills
  notes, 284-285, 290
  taking tests, 222-223
Subject card, 272-273
Subject of the sentence, 50, 59, 128
  nouns as, 86-87
  pronouns as, 102-103
Suffixes, 28-29
Synonyms, 40-41, 346-347

Table of contents, 274-275
Talking with others
  about a book, 16
  conversations, 10-11
  introductions, 6-7
  taking messages, 14-15

on the telephone, 13-14
  See also Speaking and listening skills.
Tall tale, 122-123,
Telephone skills
  taking messages, 14-15
  talking on, 12-13
Tests, following directions for, 222-223
Thank-you notes, 252-253
*Their, there,* and *they're,* 108-109
Thinking clearly, 257-267
  advertisements, 264
  facts, 258-262, 266-267
  generalizations, 263-265
  listening to commercials, 264-265
  opinions, 258-262
*This, that, these, those,* 177-178
Title card, 272-273
Titles
  of books, 270-275
  capitalization of, 302-303, 305
  of persons, 296, 297, 304
  quotation marks with, 302-303
  of stories, 163, 167
  underlining of, 302-303, 305, 321, 323, 325
  of written works, 277-278
Topic sentence
  in descriptions, 195
  in *how* paragraphs, 230-231
  in paragraphs, 66-67, 75
  in reports, 287
  writing, steps in, 70-71

*un-* (prefix), 26-27
Underlining, titles of books, 302-303, 321

Verbs, 127-153
  action, 130-132
  basic form, with plural subject, 136-141
  *be,* forms of, 130-132, 148
  that change their form, 140-143, 150-151

in contractions, 144–146
helping, 133–135, 140–141, 149
main, 133, 135
negatives, using correctly, 147, 151, 153
in past time, 139–141, 150, 153
in present time, 136–138, 149, 153
-s form, with singular subject, 136–137
that say that something *is*, 130–132
that say that something *does*, 130–132

*W* questions, 122–123
  in newspaper stories, 166
  in story telling, 117
Word Bank for Writers, 341–345
Words, 19–31.
  adding prefixes to, 26–27
  adding suffixes to, 28–29
  borrowed, 22–23
  clipped, 24
  compound, 25
  that describe, 192, 194
  echoic, 20–21, 208–209
  finding clues to meanings of, 38–39, 44–45
  first, capitalization of, 300–301
  homophones, 46, 339–340
  from sounds, 20–21, 208–209
  *See also* Dictionary.
Writing. *See* Descriptions; *How* paragraph; Letters, Friendly; Paragraphs; Prewriting; Revising; Reports; Stories.

*you*
  as understood subject, 55
  verb forms with, 137

ZIP code, 248

## Editorial Credits

Executive Editor for Language Arts:
  Bonnie L. Dobkin
Director of Language Arts:
  Carolyn McConnell
Associate Editor: Bernice Rappoport
Assistant Editor: Roslyn Weinstein
Rights and Permissions:
  Irma Rosenberg, Betty Godvik

Executive Editor: Kathleen Laya
Managing Editor: Geraldine Macsai
Senior Designer: Mary MacDonald
Design and Art Supervision: Dale Bēda, Donna Cook, Laima T. Gecas, Diane McKnight, Luis Ramirez
Cover Design: Mary MacDonald and Laima T. Gecas

## Acknowledgments

Atheneum Publishers, Inc.: For "Wind Song" from *I Feel the Same Way* by Lilian Moore; copyright © 1967 by Lilian Moore. For "Secret Hand" from *A Word or Two with You* by Eve Merriam; copyright © 1981 by Eve Merriam. A. S. Barnes & Company, Inc.: For "A Funny Man" by Natalie Joan from *Barnes Book of Nursery Verse*, compiled by Barbara Ireson; Copyright © 1960 by A. S. Barnes & Company; all rights reserved. Doubleday & Company, Inc.: For "Only My Opinion" from *Goose Grass Rhymes* by Monica Shannon; copyright 1930 by Doubleday & Company, Inc. For an excerpt from "The Sounds We Hear" by Craig Hurley from *Best in Children's Books;* copyright © 1958 by Nelson Doubleday, Inc. E. P. Dutton & Co., Inc.: For "Galoshes" from *Stories to Begin On* by Rhoda W. Bacmeister; copyright 1940 by E. P. Dutton & Co., Inc.; renewal copyright © 1968 by Rhoda W. Bacmeister. Harcourt Brace Jovanovich, Inc. For "Fog" from *Chicago Poems* by Carl Sandburg; copyright 1916 by Holt, Rinehart and Winston, Inc.; copyright 1944 by Carl Sandburg. Harper and Row, Publishers, Inc.: For "There Isn't Time" from *Eleanor Farjeon's Poems for Children* by Eleanor Farjeon; copyright © 1961 by Eleanor Farjeon. For "Spring" from *Out in the Dark and Daylight* by Aileen Fisher; copyright © 1980 by Aileen Fisher. For a text excerpt from *Owl at Home*, written and illustrated by Arnold Lobel; copyright © 1975 by Arnold Lobel. Florence Parry Heide: For "Rocks;" copyright © 1969 by Florence Parry Heide. Alfred A. Knopf, Inc.: For "The Lizard," from *A Child's Bestiary* by John Gardner; copyright © 1977 by Boskydell Artists, Ltd. For "Dream Dust," from *The Panther and the Lash: Poems of Our Times* by Langston Hughes; copyright 1947 by Langston Hughes. Little, Brown and Company: For an excerpt from "The Duck" from *Verses from 1929 On* by Ogden Nash; copyright 1936 by the Curtiss Publishing Company; first appeared in the *Saturday Evening Post*, 1936. Macmillan Publishing Company: For "Night" from *Collected Poems* by Sara Teasdale; copyright 1930 by Sara Teasdale Filsinger, renewed 1958 by Morgan Guaranty Trust Co. Of New York. Harold Ober Associates: For "City" from *The Langston Hughes Reader;* copyright © 1958 by Langston Hughes. Poets and Writers Inc.: For "Here Comes the Band," by William Cole copyright © 1960 by William Cole. G. P. Putnam's Sons: For "Brooms," from *Everything & Anything* by Dorothy Aldis: copyright 1925, 1926, 1927; renewed © 1953, 1954, 1955 by Dorothy Aldis. Marian Reiner: For an excerpt from "What in the World" from *There Is No Rhyme for Silver* by Eve Merriam; copyright © by Eve Merriam. Paul R. Reynolds, Inc.: For "Hokku: In The Falling Snow" by Richard Wright; copyright © by Richard Wright. Every effort has been made to trace the ownership of all copyrighted material found in this book and to make full acknowledgment for its use. Portions of the material in this book were previously published under the title *Building English Skills*, © McDougal, Littell & Company.

## Illustrations

Karen Ackoff, 46, 100, 106, 292, 319; JoAnna Adamska, 306; Elizabeth Allen, 53, 55, 65, 116, 117, 145, 157, 160, 199, 297; Cheryl Arnemann, 104; Steve Bates, 136, 142, 286, 287, 289; Wayne Bonnett, 38, 71, 120, 132, 284, 302; Suzanne Clee, 276, 321; Rich Cooley, 28, 29, 35, 42, 43; Carolyn Croll, 140; David Cunningham, 20, 76, 166, 171, 180; Len Ebert, 3, 6, 9, 26, 34, 54, 56–57, 66, 102, 107, 112, 119, 123, 129, 133, 134, 138, 152, 184, 192, 206, 218, 224, 301; Larry Frederick, 200, 241; Tom Garcia, 77; Linda Gist, 176, 259, 261, 263; Lydia Halverson, 250, 252; Richard Harvey, 91, 109; Greg Hergert, 10, 12, 13; Ann Iosa, 21, 22, 23, 25, 45 (bottom), 78, 137, 147, 158, 205, 207, 264; Ken Izzi, 217, 249 (bottom); Lauri Jordan, 69, 124, 141, 164; Dorothy Kavka, 266, 273; Jane Kendall, 51; Robert Korta, 86, 96, 235, 236; Barbara Lanza, 165; Karen Loccisano, 8, 11, 41; Kip Lott, 39, 174, 179, 193, 195, 197, 303; Diane McKnight, 130; Kim Mulkey, 60, 291, 324; Nancy Munger, 146, 175, 183; Rodica Prato, 27, 30; Leslie Robin, 45 (top); Jackie Rodgers, 177, 198, 314; Dennis Schofield, 178, 246, 247, 278, 283; Mary Sherman, 24; Dan Siculan, 88, 89, 92, 93, 101, 122, 204, 211, 221, 298; Susan Snider, 108, 208, 265; Krystyna Stasiak, 83; Steve Sullivan, 90, 181, 209, 216, 260; Pat Traub, 64, 121, 139, 163; Deb Troyer, 212, 249, 270, 277, 279, 312; John Walter Jr., 228, 229, 230, 231, 233; Linda Weller, 16, 40; Lane Yerkes, 188, 317. Cursive writing by PenGraphics.

## Photo Credits

FPG International: Dennis Hallinan, 190; Tom Tracy, 308. H. Armstrong Roberts/ Camerique Photography: 114. The Image Bank: Barbara Kreye, 280; Alvis Upitis, 214. The Image Works: Mark Antman, 294. International Stock Photos: George Ancona, 48. Magnum Photos: Martin J. Dain, 18. Photo Researchers, Inc.: Richard Hutchings, 172. Taurus Photos: Alec Duncan, 32; Pam Hasegawa, 98. West Light: Cradoc Bagshaw, 202. Jim Cronk: 154, 226. Tom Myers: 84. Frank Oberle, 62. Elliott Varner Smith: 126. Jim Whitmer: 4, 242, 256, 268.

(Continued from Student Letter page.)

Henderson, Rose, "Growing Old."
Hughes, Langston, "Dream Dust," *The Panther and the Lash: Poems of Our Times;* "City," *The Langston Hughes Reader.* ▸*The Dream Keeper and Other Poems*
Kennedy, X. J., "Mixed-up Kid," *The Forgetful Wishing Well.* ▸*Knock at a Star*
Kuskin, Karla, "Catherine," "The Question," *Dogs and Dragons, Trees and Dreams.* ▸*Any Me I Want to Be*
Lofting, Hugh, from *The Story of Doctor Dolittle.* ▸*Doctor Dolittle's Garden*
Merriam, Eve, "Shh," "Secret Hand," *A Word or Two with You;* "What in the World," *There Is No Rhyme for Silver.* ▸*Independent Voices*
Milne, A. A., from *Winnie the Pooh.* ▸*The World of Christopher Robin*
Moore, Lilian, "Wind Song," *I Feel the Same Way.* ▸*See My Lovely Poison Ivy*
Navaho Song, "My Great Corn Plants."
Prelutsky, Jack, "Fish," *Zoo Doings;* "Henrietta Snetter," *The New Kid on the Block.* ▸*The Snopp on the Sidewalk and Other Poems*
Reeves, James, "W," *James Reeves: The Complete Poems.*
Rossetti, Christina, "Clouds." ▸*Poems for Young Readers*
Stevenson, Robert Louis, "The Swing," *A Child's Garden of Verses.*
Stoutenburg, Adrien, "Rain," *The Things That Are.* ▸*American Tall Tales*
Teasdale, Sara, "Night," *Collected Poems.* ▸*Stars Tonight*
Viorst, Judith, "Since Hanna Moved Away," *If I Were in Charge of the World and Other Worries: Poems for Children and Their Parents.* ▸*The Tenth Good Thing About Barney*
Wilde, Oscar, from *Little Hans: The Devoted Friend.*
Wright, Richard, "Hokku: In The Falling Snow."

▸An additional work by the author